Liturgy in Ancient Jerusalem

by John F. Baldovin, S.J.
Professor of Liturgy, University of Notre Dame, U.S.A.

THE ALCUIN CLUB and the GROUP FOR RENEWAL OF WORSHIP (GROW)

The Alcuin Club, which exists to promote the study of Christian liturgy in general and of Anglican liturgy in particular, traditionally published a single volume annually for its members. This ceased in 1986. Similarly, GROW was responsible from 1975 to 1986 for the quarterly 'Grove Liturgical Studies'. Since the beginning of 1987 the two have sponsored a Joint Editorial Board to produce quarterly 'Joint Liturgical Studies'. Full details of the current series of Joint Liturgical Studies are set out in the end-pages of this Study.

THE COVER PICTURE

depicts the Madaba Mosaic map of Jerusalem

First Impression March 1989
ISSN 0951-2667
ISBN 1 85174 107 0

 **GROVE BOOKS LIMITED**
Bramcote   Nottingham   NG9 3DS

CONTENTS

AUTHOR'S ACKNOWLEDGEMENT

I put on record my gratitude to the members of my doctoral seminar of Spring 1988: Father Auxentios, Susan Hames, Lizette Larson-Miller. Peter McGrath, and Jan Robitscher, as well as to my colleagues at the Jesuit School of Theology at Berkeley.

John F. Baldovin

Introduction

A. THE IMPORTANCE OF THE JERUSALEM LITURGY

Christian worship has never been merely an abstract set of prayers and rubrics which are eternally valid for all times and places, but rather the manner in which people in specific historical, social, and cultural circumstances express their faith through symbolic ritual. In order to appreciate this necessarily inculturated nature of liturgy it is crucial that we attempt to understand a people's way of praying as a whole, as a kind of liturgical system. This is a project which has already been initiated by a number of scholars.[1]

This brief study will investigate the liturgy of Jerusalem, a church which especially in its classic period had a far-reaching and permanent effect on the rest of Christianity. In this sense Jerusalem's liturgy represents far more than just one system of worship among many. The liturgy of Jerusalem is a vital link in the many chains of development that emerge from Christian antiquity. And if it is appropriate to say that all cities served a symbolic function in pre-industrial society, then with a certain amount of confidence one can argue that Jerusalem was hyper-symbolic.

Jerusalem was (and remains) an idea, a dream. For the Jews, who were legally expelled from the city throughout the period covered by this Study, Jerusalem was a remembrance of things past and a hope for things to come; for the Christians Jerusalem was a new 'holy of holies;' for Muslims it was to become the third holy city after Mecca and Medina. As a symbolic centre this holy city (Gk. *Hagia polis*, hence the adjective hagiopolite) drew large numbers of pilgrims from throughout the Christian world, pilgrims who were to return to their homes liturgically inspired by 'the way they do it' in the holy places.[2] Thus the Jerusalem liturgy provides an important key to a number of developments elsewhere, as we shall see throughout the course of this Study.

In addition to transient pilgrims Jerusalem also attracted more permanent settlers like Jerome, the Elder and Younger Melanias, Rufinus, and even the

---

[1] For example, René Bornert, *La reforme protestante de culte à Strasbourg au XVIme siècle (1523-1598): approches sociologiques et interprétation théologique* (Leiden, 1981); Josef Schmitz, *Gottesdienst im altchristlichen Mailand: Eine liturgiewissenschaftliche Untersuchung über Initiation und Messfeier während des Jahres zur Zeit des Bischofs Ambrosius (+397),(Theophaneia 25*, Köln-Bonn, 1975); John F. Baldovin, *The Urban Character of Christian Worship: The Origins, Development and Meaning of Stational Liturgy,* (Orientalia Analecta Christiana 228, Rome, 1987).

For the socio-cultural setting of the early Byzantine city, see A. H. M. Jones, *The Greek City from Alexandra to Justinian,* (Oxford Univ. Press, Oxford, repr. 1979).

[2] On pilgrimage, see E. D. Hunt, *Holy Land Pilgrimage in the Later Roman Empire AD 312-460,* (Oxford Univ, Press, Oxford, 1984); also P. Maraval, 'Liturgie et pélèrinage durant les premiers siècles de christianisme,' *La Maison-Dieu* 170 (1987), pp.7-28.

Empress Eudocia, exiled wife of Theodosius II, who were to make the city and its environs their earthly dwelling place even as they hoped for one that was better.

The accounts of pilgrims and settlers, as well as the numerous documents that come down to us from the city's own liturgical tradition, combine to make Jerusalem the richest source for materials on Christian worship in the period of Late Antiquity.

For this reason alone liturgy in Jerusalem deserves to be studied as a whole. Therefore instead of adopting the more common method of analyzing a liturgical unit (eucharist or initiation for example) chronologically and across various traditions (comparatively), we shall here attempt an overview of Jerusalem's liturgy as a system within the context of the history of the city itself, for it is only when we can understand how the aspects of liturgical life relate to one another that we can begin to answer that most important (and rarely asked) question in the field of worship: what did all of this mean for the people who participated in it?

B. SCOPE

This study covers some three hundred years from the conversion of Constantine (312) and the consequent toleration and triumph of Christianity to the fall of Jerusalem (638) in the impressive sweep of the Islamic conquest under the Caliph Omar. This Byzantine period of hagiopolite history is rich in sources, including the church historian Eusebius, the bishops Cyril and John, pilgrimage accounts (especially that of Egeria), the homilies of Hesychius, letters and lives of a number of ascetics like Melania the Younger and Jerome, two very important lectionaries (the Armenian and the Georgian), and of course the Liturgy of St. James. In addition numerous archaeological remains, as well as artifacts and other works of art, enhance our understanding of the cultural setting and our reconstruction of what the hagiopolite liturgy might have been like.[1]

In terms of content we shall survey the entire urban worship life to the extent that the sources of the fourth-seventh centuries allow, beginning with the process of becoming a Christian (the catechumenate and initiation) and moving to the culmination of initiation in the central ongoing Christian ritual act, the eucharist. There we shall pay particular attention to the hagiopolite eucharistic prayer (Gk. *anaphora*, meaning 'the lifting up', 'the (prayer of) offering') of St. James and its relation to the prayer described in the mystagogical catecheses of Cyril. A consideration of the nature and content of daily prayer (the divine office) follows, and the whole is concluded with a chapter on the nature and development of the liturgical year at Jerusalem, with particular reference to the stational character of hagiopolite liturgy.

---

[1] For a description of the liturgical sources, see Gabriel Bertonière, *The Hostorical Development of the Greek Easter Vigil and Related Services in the Greek Church*, (Orientalia Christiana Analecta 193, Rome, 1972), pp.12-18; also see the exhaustive annotated bibliography from 1960-1979 by Charles (Athanase) Renoux, 'Hierosolymitana', *Archiv für Liturgiewissenschaft* 23 (1981), pp.1-29, 149-175.

C. SETTING

In the Byzantine period (321-638) Jerusalem was a provincial city with little political, economic or military importance. In fact, until the Council of Chalcedon (451) Jerusalem was officially part of the ecclesiastical province of Caesarea. As we have already noted, however, it had a considerable symbolic importance for Christians. The Roman military *colonia*, Aelia Capitolina, built after the destruction of the city by the Emperor Hadrian (135) had a circumference of only *ca.* 3.5 km. According to fifth century Greek church historians, Eudocia extended the walls to include the south-western area of the city which Christians called Sion. The circumference was enlarged to a little over 4 km. Hence this was not at all a large town by modern standards. In the traditional manner of the Roman *colonia* two main thoroughfares, the *cardo maximus* (N-S) and the *cardo decumanus* (EW), intersected the city with a major forum and several temples near the intersection.[1] Colonnades lined the *cardo maximus*, as is apparent from the sixth century floor mosaic of Jerusalem and Palestine at Madaba in Jordan.[2] The town within the walls was largely composed of hills, one of which was the abandoned Temple Mount, where Herod's temple had been destroyed in 70. Although the Jews attempted to rebuild on this site with the encouragement of the Emperor Julian (361-363), they quickly ceased work with the latter's death. Nothing was constructed on the Temple Mount until after the Arab conquest.

For Christians the most important places in the city were: 1) the complex of buildings that included the Holy Sepulchre and Golgotha; and 2) a large basilica called Sion in the quarter of the same name, now called the Armenian Quarter. Both building projects took place in the course of the fourth century. The first was begun at the initiative of Constantine himself.[3] This Holy Sepulchre-Golgotha area consisted of several shrines and a basilica within a walled precinct. The complex of buildings faced toward the East on the *cardo maximus*. It was entered through a monumental gate. A glance at the plan on page 10 will show that open-air courts connected the whole precinct and that it contained a basilica, called the Martyrium, over the place where Christ's cross was discovered (1), a rotunda (2) covering the tomb (6) of Christ, a small chapel (5) to the south of Golgotha (4), and a baptistery (7). Legend naturally accumulated about the

---

[1] See the map on p.9.

[2] See M. Avi-Yonah, *The Mahada Mosaic Map,* (Jerusalem, 1954); also Yoram Tsafrir, 'Jerusalem', *Reällexikon für byzantinsche Kunst* III, pp.575-588.

[3] For a description of the building process and results, see Eusebius, *The Life of Constantine* III:25-40, translated in John Wilkinson, ed., *Egeria's Travels,* 2nd ed., (Warminster, 1981), pp.164-171.

For the Holy Sepulchre-Golgotha complex, see Charles Coüasnon, *The Church of the Holy Sepulchre in Jerusalem,* (London, 1974). For the lay-out of the city and its buildings, see Tsafrir, 'Jerusalem' pp.525-616; also B. Bagatti, *The Church From the Gentiles in Palestine,* (Jerusalem, 1971), pp.151-237. John Wilkinson provides a most helpful gazetteer in his *Jerusalem Pilgrims Before the Crusades,* (Warminster, 1974), pp.149-178.

entire site which eventually assimilated Temple legends about the burial place of Adam and the mount where Abraham was to have sacrificed Isaac. The whole complex was thus a virtual goldmine for pilgrims and was well suited to the liturgical needs of a community that wished to worship in the holiest places Christianity knew. The arrangement that obtained during the Byzantine period was completely changed by the destruction of the complex by the Fatimid Caliph Hakim (1009) and the rebuilding under the Crusaders in the twelfth century.

Other churches in and around the city can be described more briefly. Sion was the original meeting place of the post-Easter Christian community. Eventually both the site of the Last Supper as well as the event of Pentecost were associated with it. Other fourth century foundations included: Eleona, a basilica atop the Mount of Olives to the East of the city[1], the *Imbomon* (Gk. for 'Hillock,' a shrine of the Ascension located nearby the Eleona and built at the instigation of the Roman matron Poimenia ca. 390, and a church called 'graceful' by Egeria, located near the base of the Mount of Olives.[2] Two other churches fill out the scenario for the fourth century hagiopolite liturgical calendar. The first was the basilica at Bethlehem, built over the site of Christ's birth by Constantine and consecrated in 333[3]; and the second the Lazarium, at Bethany where, Jesus raised Lazarus, about three km. east of the city over the Mount of Olives.

The fifth century was a period of great expansion in ecclesiastical construction in and around Jerusalem. Besides a number of monasteries which sprang up on and around the Mount of Olives and at Bethlehem, important churches include: a martyrium in honour of St. Stephen, whose relics were discovered in 415, dedicated in 439; St. Peter's, also called the House of Caiaphas in the neighbourhood of Sion; and a church by the Probatic Pool, just north of the Temple Mount and dedicated first to the birth of the Virgin Mary and later to her mother, St. Anne. Thus, in a sense, ecclesiastical construction in the fifth century was dedicated to filling in the story of the events associated with the holy places.[4]

One last church should be mentioned, namely the Nea, or New St. Mary's, built by Justinian in the sixth century and dedicated on November 21, which was to become the major Byzantine feast of the Presentation of Mary in the Temple. Recent archaeological excavations have pinpointed its location to an area just south of the Temple Mount.[5] It was destroyed in the Persian conquest of 614 and never rebuilt, either from lack of funds or possibly because it was not associated with an event in the life of Christ.

---

[1] Eusebius, *Life of Constantine* III:41.
[2] Egeria 36:1.
[3] Eusebius, *Life of Constantine* III:41-43.
[4] See, Hunt, *Holy Land Pilgrims, pp.155-179.*
[5] See Procopius, *The Buildings of Justinian,* in H. B. Dewing, ed., *Loeb Classical Library: Procopius VII,* (Cambridge, MA, 1961), pp.343-349; see also F. E. Peters, *Jerusalem: The Holy City in the Eyes of Chroniclers, Visitors, Pilgrims and Prophets from the Days of Abraham to the Beginnings of Mordern Times,* (Princeton Univ. Press, Princeton, 1985), pp.162-166.

Reprinted with permission, the Pontifical Oriental Institute Press, Rome—from Orientalia Christiana Analecta 228 (Rome, 1987).

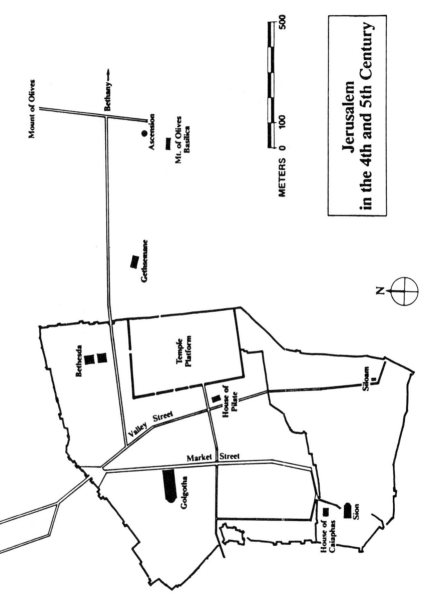

Mount of Olives

Bethany →

Ascension

Mt. of Olives Basilica

Gethsemane

Bethesda

Temple Platform

Valley Street

House of Pilate

Siloam

Market Street

Golgotha

House of Caiaphas

Sion

N

METERS 0   100   500

Jerusalem in the 4th and 5th Century

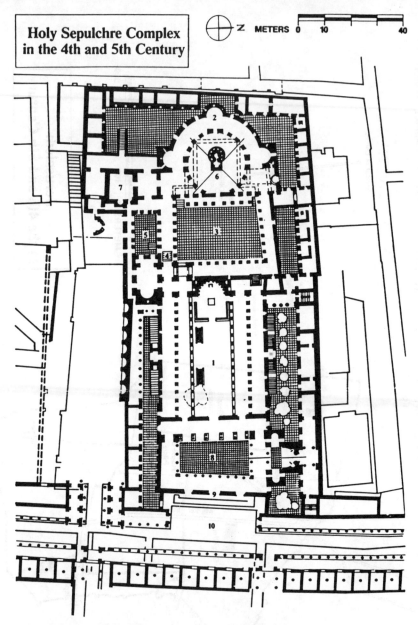

Holy Sepulchre Complex in the 4th and 5th Century

METERS 0 10 40

1. Constantine's Basilica (Martyrium)
2. Rotunda of Resurrection (Anastasis)
3. Forecourt at the Cross
4. The Cross (Golgotha)
5. Chapel Behind the Cross
6. Tomb of Christ
7. Baptistery
8. Forecourt of Basilica
9. Main Entrance (Propylacum)
10. Market Street (Cardo Maximus)

Reprinted with permission, the Pontifical Oriental Institute Press, Rome—from Orientalia Christiana Analecta 228 (Rome, 1987).

after Charles Couasnon

2. Initiation

A. THE CATECHUMENATE

The only extant complete set of Lenten catechetical lectures in the early church comes to us from Cyril of Jerusalem.[1] In the fourth century the catechumenate was still in a considerable state of flux due to the radically changed political and social status of Christians. Formerly the decisive commitment to Christian faith consisted in entrance into the catechumenate itself, as in the *Apostolic Tradition* ascribed to Hippolytus.[2] But now the decisive act seems to have been the decision to embark upon the final stage of the catechumenate at the beginning of Lent. As to the length of the catechumenate itself in the fourth century we have no certain evidence. In any case by this time many if not most adults postponed initiation as long as possible, presumably to postpone having to submit to the rigours of the fully Christian life and the discipline of public penance should they fail.

Hagiopolite sources for the last half of the fourth century show clearly that the period of final preparation for baptism began on the first day of Lent[3], a Monday, with an inscription of the names of the candidates by the bishop after he had examined them as to their motives and probity of life.[4] In Egeria's account each candidate is presented to the bishop by a godparent (*patribus, matribus*). Some

---

[1] Cyril was the bishop of Jerusalem from 350 to 387, although exiled several times over the Arian controversy. For biographical information and commentary, see A. Paulin, *Saint Cyrille de Jérusalem, Catéchète*, (Lex Orlandi 29, Paris, 1959); Edward Yarnold, 'Cyrillus von Jerusalem', *Theologische Real-Encyclopädie* 8 (Berlin, 1981, pp.261-266; Johannes Quasten, *Patrology* III, (Utrecht, 1960), pp.362-363. Cyril's Procatechesis and eighteen catechetical lectures (PG 33:331-1064) are translated in *Nicene and Post-Nicene Fathers*, 2nd series, vol. VII, (repr. Eerdmans, Grand Rapids, 1978), pp.1-143. These lectures were delivered while Cyril was still a presbyter in 348.

[2] See Geoffrey J. Cuming, *Hippolytus: A Text for Students*, (Grove Liturgical Study 8, Bramcote, Notts., 1976), p.15.

[3] See Georg Kretschmar, 'Die Geschichte des Taufgottesdienstes in der alten Kirche', *Leitourgia*, vol. 5 (Kassel, 1970), pp.147-152.

[4] Cyril, *Procat.* 4; Egeria 45:2. For details as to the dating of Egeria's account, see Wilkinson, *Egeria*, pp.3-8, 27-30; and Pierre Maraval, *Égérie: Journal de Voyage*, (Sources Chrétiennes 296, Paris, 1982), pp.15-117. It has been established with some scholarly consensus that Egeria (rather than the names Etheria or Sylvia previously given) most probably travelled the Eastern Mediterranean in the years 381-384 and came from Galicia in North-Western Spain. Wilkinson's translation (p.143) mistakes the second day of the week (Monday) for the second day of Lent.

testimony to the candidate's fitness is necessary as a stranger can be accepted only with difficulty (45.4). Cyril gives no clear indication as to when the course of catechetical instructions is completed except to say that the feast of Easter (pascha) is at hand (Cat. XVII.20; XVIII.32). Egeria, on the other hand, reporting some thirty years later, claims that the catecheses are all given before the beginning of Great (Holy) Week because of the length of the ceremonies during that final week of preparation for the paschal feast (46.5).

The content of the Lenten catechetical instructions in Cyril is mainly an explication of the creed (Cat. IV-XVIII) with a general introduction (Procatechesis) and three lectures (Cat. I-III) of a preparatory nature on baptism. This syllabus is corroborated by the series of readings found in the Armenian Lectionary, which corresponds exactly to Cyril's with the exception of a nineteenth reading (I Timothy 3.14-16).[1] This raises the possibility that the eighteenth of Cyril's lectures was originally two lectures, since the content of the last half of the final lecture corresponds to the reading from I Timothy. Egeria, however, describes the hagiopolite syllabus differently:

'His (the bishop's) subject is God's Law; during the forty days he goes through the whole Bible, beginning with Genesis, and first relating the literal meaning of each passage, then interpreting its spiritual meaning . . . After five weeks' teaching they receive the Creed, whose content he explains in the same way as he explained the Scriptures, first literally and then spiritually'. (46.23)

Is Egeria faithfully reporting hagiopolite practice? We know that it was not uncommon in the fourth century to deliver catechetical lectures on the scriptures.[2] But, given the evidence of a full set of catecheses in Cyril, matched by an equal number in the fifth century Armenian Lectionary, as well as the fact that Cyril's description of the content of Scripture (Cat. IV. 33-37)does not presuppose previous lectures on the subject[3],it could well be that Egeria had confused

---

[1] In 1961 Athanase (Charles) Renoux published a French translation of the newly discovered and oldest version of the Armenian Lectionary, which reproduced the feasts, commemorations, readings, stations, and a number of rubrics for the church at Jerusalem in the years 417-439. See 'Un manuscrit du vieux lectionnaire arménien de Jérusalem', *Le Muséon* 74 (1961), pp.361-385; for the Armenian and the French translation of three important manuscripts (including Paris BN Arm. 44 and Erevan 385) see Renoux, *Le Codex Arménien Jérusalem 121, Introduction* (Patrologia Orientalis 35:1, Paris 1969), pp.5-197; *Texte* (PO 36:2, Paris, 1971), pp.211-373.

[2] For example, Basil the Great, *On the Hexaemeron*, (PG 29:3-208). For other examples, see Kretschmar, 'Geschichte des Tauffgottes-dienstes', p.162.

[3] For another view, see Thomas J. Talley, *The Origins of the Liturgical Year*, (Pueblo Publ. Co., New York, 1986), p.176. Talley argues that we do not possess all of Cyril's lectures.

the content of Jerusalem's lectures with that of another church or simply confused the timing.[1]

We have little information to go on when it comes to the question of precisely when during Lent that the lectures were given. According to Egeria ((46.3) they took place every day from 6 till 9 am in the Martyrium between the dismissal from morning prayer and the extra Lenten prayer service (Terce). But, if Cyril's lectures represent a complete series, as I have just argued they did, then they could not have been given every day. Two time-references within the lectures themselves may be of some help.

In Cat. X.14 Cyril reminds his listeners that in his Sunday sermon the day before he had commented on the phrase 'after the order of Melchizedek.' And in Cat. XIV.24 he tells them that 'yesterday' (a Sunday) he had preached on the ascension of Christ. These subjects, particularly the latter, seem to be odd subjects for Lenten Sunday homilies. At this point, however, one can turn to comparative liturgy for a possible solution. Talley has noted that there are certain relations between the lectionary of Constantinople and hagiopolite practice, especially with reference to Lazarus Saturday and Palm Sunday.[2] The Constantinopolitan lectionary for Saturdays and Sundays contains a series of course readings from the Letter to the Hebrews and the Gospel of Mark. The first reading prescribed for the Third Sunday of Lent is Heb. 4.14-5.6, which ends with the phrase that Cyril quotes in his tenth lecture. That phrase is also included in the reading for the Fourth Sunday, a passage that can also be read as alluding to the ascension of Christ. '. . . a hope that enters into the inner shrine behind the curtain where Jesus has gone on our behalf, having become a high priest . . .' (Heb. 6.19-20). One could also see a reference to the ascension of Christ in the reading for the Fifth Sunday (Heb. 9.11-14) in which Jesus is described as having entered once for all into 'the greater and perfect tent not made by hands.' Comparison with the subject matter of Cyril's letters suggests that his references were to the same readings that the Byzantine lectionary contained.

If this be the case, then we have a way of distributing Cyril's Lenten lectures. I have suggested elsewhere that the Lenten lectures were distributed according to days which did not have stational services.[3] Cyril's references to his Sunday sermons may corroborate this suggestion in that the tenth lecture would have been given on Monday of the Fourth Week of Lent (remember that the week began on

---

[1] For a recent attempt to solve this problem, especially with regard to the duration of Lent, see Maxwell Johnson, 'Reconciling Cyril and Egeria in the Catechetical process in Fourth-Century Jerusalem', in Paul Bradshaw (ed.), *Essays in Early Eastern Initiation*, (Alcuin-GROW Liturgical Study 8, Grove Books, Bramcote, Notts., 1988) pp.18-30.

[2] Yalley, *Origins*, pp.183-189.

[3] See J. F. Baldovin, *Urban Character*, pp.90-93.

a Monday not a Sunday as in the West) and the fourteenth lecture would have been given on Monday of the Fifth Week of Lent.[1]

Other factors in the conduct of the hagiopolite catechumenate come to light in the catechetical lectures of Cyril. The candidates are called *photizomenoi* (those to be enlightened, Procat.1). They have previously been called 'catechumens' (hearers Procat.6).[2] The *photizomenoi* have already carried torches in an unexplained ceremony on the first day of Lent (Procat.1,3; Cat. I.1). They undergo exorcisms by being breathed upon, apparently a fear-inspiring experience (Procat. 9, Cat. I.5). Egeria mentions (46.1) that the exorcisms took place immediately before the lectures. The *photizomenoi* also have their faces veiled. According to Cyril this prevents their minds from wandering or conjuring up unwanted thoughts (Procat.9). They are also expected to make *exomologesis* (confession) of their sins (Cat. I.5; II.19-20), but the manner of doing so is unclear. Of course they are expected to remain faithful to the lectures (Procat. 10,11) and to fast as other Christians do during Lent (Cat. III.7).[3] Cyril also alludes to the handing over of the Creed to the candidates (Cat. IV.3; V.12; XVIII.21). Egeria describes (46.2) both this practice and the repetition of the Creed by the *conpetentes* at the end of the week preceding Holy Week.

The handing over and repetition of the Creed leads to another consideration with regard to the hagiopolite catechumenate, namely secrecy the *disciplina arcani*. Cyril insists several times that what the *photizomenoi* have learned is not to be shared with outsiders, not even catechumens. This demand for secrecy extends not only to the liturgical mysteries (baptism and eucharist, Cat. XVIII.33) but also to the Creed (Cat. V.12; VI.29) and the content of the lectures themselves (Procat.12,17). Similarly Egeria mentions that the catechumens may not enter the Martyrium during the catechetical lectures (46.2). So, both sources indicate a concern for secrecy that extends beyond the liturgical rites. How widespread was such secrecy during the fourth century? Kretschmar has concluded that in terms of strict secrecy the Creed as well as many aspects of baptism and the eucharist must have been a fiction, since in the fourth century these had become public knowledge.[4] Thus the concern for secrecy may have

---

[1] Thus it seems to me that Kretschmar is incorrect in assigning the fourteenth lecture to Monday of Holy Week with the reasoning that the ascension formed the subject because the day before (Palm Sunday) the church had assembled at the Imbomon. See his 'Geschichte des Taufgottesdienstes', p.161n. and further argumentation in his 'Die frühe der jerusalemer Liturgie', *Jahrbuch für Liturgik und Hymnologie* 2 (1956), pp.37-38.

[2] Egeria (45:2) calls each candidate a *conpetens*. The Western nomenslature *competentes* (candidates) and *audientes* (hearers) thus matched the Eastern. At Rome the candidates were called *electi*. See, Heorge Gingras, *Egeria: Diary of A Pilgrimage*, (Ancient Christian Writers 38, Washington, DC, 1970), pp.250-251.

[3] On the fast at Jerusalem during Lent, see also Egeria 27:9-28:4.

[4] Kretschmar, 'Geschicte des Taufgottesdienstes', p.157. On the whole subject of the *Disciplina arcani*, see pp.154-163.

been more of an effort to impress upon the candidates an awareness of the magnitude of what they were hearing and experiencing.

A final aspect relevant to the catechumenate at Jerusalem is Cyril's frequent references to the holy places themselves. He refers to them no less than sixty-seven times in the lectures, usually appealing to them as witnesses to the truth of what he is describing. For example in Cat. X.19 he enumerates with great rhetorical flourish the testimonies of Christ. Beginning with scriptural and natural evidence he proceeds:

'The holy wood of the cross bears witness, seen among us to this day ...
Golgotha, the holy hill standing above us here bears witness to our sight.
The Holy Sepulchre bears witness ... the Mount of Olives bears witness'.

In other words, effective pedagogue that he is, Cyril employs what is familiar and at hand to instruct his listeners.[1] And what was at hand in Jerusalem made very food catechetical material indeed.

B. THE RITES OF INITIATION

The solemn rites of initiation in the fourth and fifth century Jerusalem liturgy took place at the great vigil of Easter. Our sources come from Cyril, Egeria, and the Armenian Lectionary.[2] Cyril's information is provided *via* an important new fourth century form, the mystagogy, of which we possess three other significant witnesses. Ambrose of Milan, John Chrysostom, and Theodore of Mopsuestia.[3] We may have more examples of mystagogy than pre-initiatory catechesis in the fourth century because rites of initiation may well have differed far more significantly than the catechetical syllabus.[4]

---

[1] For other examples, see Cat.IV:10; XIII:4, 38; XIV:14. The citation above in Cat.X:19 shows that by this time the wood of the cross had been discovered. Apparently this had not been the case when Eusebius wrote his *Life of Constantine* (337-340) nor when the Bordeaux Pilgrim visited the holy places (333).

[2] In this case Cyril's mystagogical (post-initiatory) catechesis. For the text in Greek and R. W. Church's English translation, see F. L. Cross, *St. Cyril of Jerusalem: Lectures on the Christian Sacraments*, (repr., St. Vladimir's Seminary Press, Crestwood, NY, 1977). I follow here the traditional attribution of the five mystagogical catecheses to Cyril rather than his successor, John II (387-417). For details and arguments, see A. Piedagnel, *Cyrille de Jérusalem: Catéchèses Mystagogiques*, (Sources Chretiennes 126, Paris, 1966), pp.18-40; Edward Yarnold, 'The Authorship of the Mystagogical Catecheses Attributed to Cyril of Jerusalem'. *The Heythrop Journal* 19 (1978), pp.143-161. The best solution to a number of problems presented by discrepancies between the catechetical and mystagogical lectures is to argue that the latter stem from the end of Cyril's episcopate (some thirty-five to forty years after the former) and may perhaps have been edited by John (see Kretschmar, 'Fruhe Geschicte', p.27).

[3] The lectures of all four preachers can conveniently be found in Edward Yarnold, *The Awe-Inspiring Rites of Initiation*, (St. Paul Publications, Slough, 1971). For an exhaustive commentary and analysis, see Hugh Riley, *Christian Initiation* (Studies in Christian Antiquity 17, Consortium Press, Washington, DC, 1974).

[4] See Kretschmar, 'Geschichte des Taufgottesdienstes', pp.163-165.

A series of five mystagogical catecheses has been attributed to Cyril. This raises some problems since Cyril himself (Cat. XVIII.33) seems to indicate that lectures will be given every day of the week following Paschal baptism. Likewise Egeria (47.1) states that lectures are given each day during the Easter octave. On the other hand one early manuscript of the Armenian Lectionary (Erevan 985) indicates five readings for the mystagogies, and two other manuscripts for the same lectionary (Paris 44 and Jer.Arm. 121) provide four readings.

It is fairly easy to account for the last stage of this evolution. The solution comes from paying attention to the stational arrangement. After the discovery of the relics of St. Stephen and their deposition at the diaconicon of Sion (415), the hagiopolite stational pattern was re-arranged to include a station at the diaconicon on Tuesday of the Easter octave, replacing the earlier station, the Martyrium, on that day.[1] This re-arrangement most likely inspired dropping one of the mystagogical lectures since it would have been difficult to hold a stational eucharist and have a mystagogical lecture both on the same day in widely separated places as the mystagogical lectures were always held in the Anastasis. By the same token the number of lectures may have been reduced from seven to five in the first place because the distribution of stational churches for the octave was only in an embryonic stage when Cyril gave his Lenten catechetical lectures (348-350).[2] Thus we most probably possess all of Cyril's mystagogical catecheses for *ca.* 380-385.

Cyril begins his exposition of the rites and their meaning with a statement of pedagogical method that has timeless relevance:

'. . . knowing well that seeing is far more persuasive than hearing, I waited till this season, that, finding you more open to the influence of my words from this your experience, I might take and lead you to the brighter and more fragrant meadow of this present paradise.' (MC I.1)

He continues by commenting on the ceremonies that immediately precede baptism itself. The candidates are led into the dark vestibule of the baptistery.[3] There, facing toward the West, they stretch forth a hand and renounce Satan, his works, his pomps, and his service. The West symbolizes darkness and evil; Cyril likens Satan to the Egyptians who pursued the Israelites right up to the Red Sea (MC I.23). Then the candidates are turned toward the East and 'there is opened to you the paradise of God, which he planted toward the East' (MC I.9). The

---

[1] See Renoux, *Jer. Arm. 121*, pp.177-178.

[2] Similarly Yarnold argues that Egeria, when she reports that the mystagogies were held daily, means that they took place 'on those days in Easter week on which it is possible to hold a mystagogical assembly in the Anastasis'. 'Authorship', p.155.

[3] The baptistery seems to have consisted of four rooms: 1) a vestibule which faced toward the West and ran the length of the building; 2 and 3) two side rooms for the disrobing and pre-baptismal anointing of the men and women; 4) the baptistery proper with the font. For a sketch and further description, see Kretschmar, 'Geschichte des Taufgottesdienstes', p.205.

doors to the baptistery proper were most probably opened at this point creating a sharp contrast to the darkened vestibule. Then they make a simple profession of faith. 'I believe in the Father, and in the Son, and in the Holy Spirit, and in one baptism of repentance' (MC I.9). It is difficult to tell whether this was the full profession or a shorthand form of it. The phrase 'and in one baptism of repentance' is not found in any other fourth century source.[1] Thus the first mystagogy ends with the candidates on the threshold of their baptism.

The candidates are then led into separate rooms for disrobing, a practical necessity which receives a good deal of comment from Cyril. The naked candidates imitate Christ naked on the cross. They are to recall Adam, but, like Adam before the Fall, they are unashamed in their nakedness (MC II.2). The First Adam/Second Adam typology may well be an index of the recovery of Pauline theology found in all of the fourth century mystagogues.[2]

Next the candidates are anointed head-to-toe with exorcized oil. Cyril alone of the fourth century mystagogues employs the term 'exorcized oil' (MC II.3), although it had been used before in the third century to describe the oil for this anointing.[3] Cyril's use of the term here signals an important shift from the pre-baptismal anointing found in the Syrian and Egyptian traditions up to this point.[4] These traditions lacked a post-baptismal anointing. The pre-baptismal anointing symbolized the candidate's identification with Christ in the Jordan-event and thus his messianic and priestly role. Winkler has pointed out that this shift in hagiopolite practice connotes a movement toward identification with the death and burial of Christ instead.[5] A post-baptismal anointing is still lacking in John Chrysostom's Antiochene baptismal homilies, roughly contemporary with those of Cyril. Chrysostom does, however, interpret the pre-baptismal anointing in terms of combat with the devil.[6]

For Cyril the meaning of the pre-baptismal anointing is not merely negative or exorcistic; it also symbolizes participation in the abundance of Christ, to whom the candidate has now been joined as to the 'good olive tree' (MC I.3; also Cat.

---

[1] For further commentary, see Piédagnel, *Cyrille*, pp.99-100n. Note that the phrase does recall Cyril's wording in Cat. XVIII:22.

[2] See Kretschmar, 'Geschichte des Taufgottesdienstes', p.148; Riley, *Christian Initiation*, pp.222-224; Gabrielle Winkler, 'The Original Meaning and Implication of the Pre-baptismal Anointing', *Worship* 52 (1978), pp.40-41.

[3] *Apostolic Tradition* 21.

[4] For the Syrian tradition, see Winkler, 'Pre-baptismal Anointing', pp.29-38; for the Egyptian tradition, Paul F. Bradshaw, 'Alexandrian Baptismal Practice: Eastern or Western?'

[5] Winkler, 'Pre-baptismal Anointing', p.42. As Winkler suggests, this move may have been due more to a change in fourth century baptismal theology in general than to topographical considerations peculiar to Jerusalem.

[6] John Chrysostom, 'Baptismal Homily II', in Yarnold, *Awe-Inspiring Rites*, pp.166-167.

I.5). The oil itself has the power to drive out evil for it has received an invocation (*epiclesis*) by prayer. Thus the pre-baptismal anointing is clearly polyvalent for Cyril.

Immediately after this anointing the candidates are led to 'the holy pool of divine baptism, just as Christ was carried from the Cross to the Sepulchre which is before our eyes' (MC II.4). There for a final time they are asked to profess their faith in the Trinity and then submerged three times. There is no indication of a baptismal formula here, as there is, for example, in Chrysostom and Theodore; nor is there an explicit co-ordination of the immersions with the three articles of faith as in Theodore and Ambrose.[1] Given the manner in which Cyril describes the baptismal bath, there may well have been no baptismal formula at all.[2]

Among the mystagogues Cyril alone interprets the threefold immersion not in terms of the Trinity but rather as an imitation of Christ's three-day burial. Although the analogy he draws between the candidate's baptism and the sufferings of Christ is somewhat weak, because the burial and sufferings of Christ are not exact parallels, he here provides his most profound insights into the nature of Christian initiation:

'O strange and inconceivable thing! We did not really die, we were not really buried, we were not really crucified and raised again, but our imitation (*mimesis*) was but in a figure (*eikon*), while our salvation (*soteria*) was reality (*aletheia*).' (MC II.5)

This 'theory' can be described as participation by imitation. In other words the reality of Christ's experience is communicated to the individual who symbolically imitates the pattern of that experience. Staying close to Romans 6.3-14, the text for the mystagogy, Cyril does not quite say that the newly-baptized person participate in the resurrection, for that remains in the future. Further, he affirms baptism's relation to the forgiveness of sins, adoption, and the gift of the Spirit while at the same time emphasizing that it conveys the 'counterpart' (*antitypos*) of Christ's sufferings (MC II.6).[3]

The setting of the Anastasis has also left its mark on Cyril's preaching about baptism, a fact that is further emphasized by his analogy of the neophytes' having been 'planted' together with Christ, the true vine who has 'been planted in this place' (MC II.7).[4]

---

[1] See Chrysostom, 'Baptismal Homily II'; Theodore, Baptismal Homily III'; Ambrose, 'On the Sacraments II'; in Yarnold, *Awe-Inspiring Rites*, pp.168, 201-202, 117.

[2] *Pace* Kretschmar, 'Geschichte des Taufgottesdienstes', p.202, who sees the interpretations overshadowing the formula which he thinks was probably recited.

[3] It is not easy here to differentiate what Cyril means by type and antitype. In order to stress the reality of the relation I am here translating 'antitype' as 'counterpart' instead of Church's 'emblem'. See the very helpful note of Yarnold, *Awe-Inspiring Rites*, pp.93-94.

[4] Here Christ and not the cross is the true vine, *pace* Piédagnel, *Cyrille*, p.117n; Riley, *Christian Initiation*, p.240.

The whole of the third mystagogical lecture is given to an interpretation of a single post-baptismal ceremony the anointing with chrism.[1] As we noted above, this anointing is innovative, at least as far as our knowledge of Eastern tradition is concerned. It represents an important shift in the ritualization of Christian initiation.[2] Cyril now shifts the biblical model that the neophytes have imitated from Christ's burial to his anointing with the Holy Spirit in the Jordan. Just as Christ was anointed after his baptism, the neophytes now share in that experience as well, except that in the former was a case of 'like resting upon like,' whereas the neophytes are images (eikones) of Christ (MC III.1). Cyril's primary name for the oil employed in this anointing is chrisma but he also calls it myron (aromatic oil).[3] It is applied to the forehead, ears, nostrils, and breast; and each aspect symbolizes an effect: the forehead that they may be without shame, the ears that they might receive the divine mysteries, the nostrils that they may know they are the sweet savour of Christ, and finally the breast as armour against any further assaults of the devil (MC III.4). In all of this Cyril makes it quite clear (MC III.5) that the neophytes have derived their true name from the anointed one —Christ himself.

It seems to me that Cyril has been quite selective in his commentary here, a factor which will be relevant when we consider his description of the eucharistic prayer. He fails to mention the consecration of the font, although he spoke of it in Cat. III.3. It is unlikely, given the increase in exorcistic motifs associated with initiation, that this prayer would have been dropped.[4] Cyril also fails to mention the clothing with a white garment, a practice which may be supposed from several allusions (Procat. 15; MC IV.8).[5] There is no mention of a post-baptismal imposition of hands to which he explicitly refers in Cat. XVI.26. Finally, Cyril omits any mention of the neophytes' processing to the tomb of Christ after the anointing and prior to entering the Martyrium for the celebration of the eucharist, a practice reported as unique to Jerusalem by Egeria (38.1). It seems, therefore, that Cyril was more interested in interpreting notable elements of the rite than in giving a blow-by-blow commentary on every single element in it.

---

[1] It would be anachronistic to call this rite 'confirmation' as does Yarnold, *Awe-Inspiring Rites* pp.32, 79. For a more functional and structural interpretation of the origins of confirmation in a public ceremony linking the (private) baptism with the eucharistic assembly, see Aidan Kavanagh, *Confirmation: Origins and Reform*, (Pueblo Publ. Co., New York, 1988), pp.65-72.

[2] Of course the West already had such an anointing in the third century; see *Apostolic Tradition* 22; Tertullian, *On Baptism* 7; *On the Resurrection of the Flesh* 8. For the shift in biblical imagery and its relation to exegesis of the Jordan event, see Kretschmar, 'Geschichte de Taufgottesdienstes', pp.203, 206-207.

[3] On the terminology involved, especially with regard to Syriac equivalents, see Winkler, 'Pre-baptismal Anointing', pp.26-29; also *idem.*, *Das armenische Initiationsrituale* (Orientalia Christiana Analecta 217, Rome, 1982), pp.359, 400, 417.

[4] Kretschmar, 'Geschichte de Taufgottesdienstes', p.202 suggests that the prayer may have been recited whiule the candidates were entering the baptistery proper.

[5] See Riley, *Christian Initiation*, pp.349-350.

CONCLUSION

In this chapter we have dealt with a relatively complete picture of initiation given by our sources for fourth century Jerusalem, from the inscription of names at the beginning of Lent up to the mystagogical lectures of the Easter octave. We have noted a number of insights into the nature of hagiopolite worship, the creed as catechetical syllabus, the significance of the holy places themselves for catechesis, the recovery of the Pauline death-burial imagery, an increase in exorcistic and purificatory motifs, and a re-arrangement of the sequence and number of the anointings. We must realize, as Kretschmar has pointedly argued, that late fourth century Jerusalem initiatory practice represents the term and not the beginning of a complex development that was to become a common pattern in East and West.[1]

Of course, Christian initiation does not end with the rites we have described but rather with full incorporation into Christ's body by means of the eucharist, a subject to which we now turn.

---

[1] George Kretschmar, 'Recent Research on Christian Initiation', *Studia Liturgica* 12 (1977), p.92.

3. The Eucharist

A. STRUCTURE

The eucharist is the repeatable ritual culmination of the initiation process of full incorporation into the Body of Christ. No other Christian rite has loomed so large in importance or been so controverted. Once again we are fortunate in possessing a number of sources that illuminate the practice and theology of an important element in hagiopolite liturgy.[1] This chapter will investigate these sources with a view toward a comprehensive understanding of eucharistic practice at Jerusalem.

We begin with the structure of the eucharistic liturgy itself, in particular a problem raised by Egeria's account. In describing the Sunday morning services Egeria presupposes that her correspondents are familiar with the basic structure of the eucharist. They do it in Jerusalem basically the way it is done in her native Galician home. She comments only on the differences. One difference is that there are a number of sermons, for all the presbyters present may preach, with the bishop preaching last of all (25.1). Presumably this made for a very long liturgy of the word, lasting from daybreak until around ten or eleven o'clock. Then she describes a procession from the Martyrium, where what has just been described takes place, to the Anastasis:

'And when the dismissal has taken place in the church in the way which is usual everywhere the *monazontes* (urban monks) lead the bishop with singing to the Anastasis. While they are singing and the bishop approaches, all the doors of the Anastasis are opened, and the people (not the catechumens, only the faithful) all go in. When they are all inside, the bishop enters, and passes straight inside the screen of the tomb, the cave itself. They have a Thanksgiving to God (*gratiae aguntur Deo*) and the Prayer for All (*orationem pro omnibus*); then the deacon calls every single person to bow his head, and the bishop blesses them from his place inside the screen. Then he comes out, and, as he does so, everyone comes to have his hand laid on them. Thus the dismissal (*missa*) is delayed till almost eleven or twelve o'clock.' (25.24)

The structural problem is raised by the question: What precisely is this service which takes place in the Anastasis? Arguing that prior to the fourth century the meetings for the liturgy of the word and that of the eucharist were separate, Gregory Dix saw here a movement from the Martyrium, where the liturgy of the

---

[1] These sources include: Egeria's pilgrimage diary, Cyril's fourth and fifth mystagogical catecheses and the *anaphora* (eucharistic prayer) of St. James. For a discussion of the literature of the Anaphora of St. James, see below.

word took place, to the Anastasis for the celebration of the eucharist proper.[1] In this theory, which is followed by others[2], the 'Thanksgiving' is taken to mean the eucharistic prayer while the 'Prayer for All' refers to the intercessions. In every other allusion to the eucharist, however, Egeria uses the terms *oblatio* (offering) and *offerre* (to offer) when referring to the eucharist.[3]

Another possible interpretation of the passage holds that the service in the Anastasis refers to a second celebration but of the eucharist proper; i.e. without the liturgy of the word, as one finds on Holy Thursday, Easter, and Pentecost.[4] There may have been good reasons (overflow of people?) for such duplication on special feast days, but why, one must ask, every Sunday?

A third possibility remains, namely that the service in the Anastasis consisted of a brief thanksgiving and intercession albeit with a long process of dismissal.[5] In my opinion this last is the most reasonable interpretation. In the first place we have a contemporary witness to a parallel thanksgiving after communion complete with intercessory prayer in the *Apostolic Constitutions*.[6] Second, the fusion of the word and eucharistic liturgies seems to have taken place already in the second century according to the First Apology of Justin Martyr. Third, when describing the same movement on Pentecost Egeria explicitly mentions(43.3) that the eucharist is celebrated at the Martyrium as usual (*offertur juxta consuetudinem*). Moreover, the other theories have not taken into consideration the possibility that the dismissal structure may have been far more elaborate than is ordinarily supposed.[7]

---

[1] Gregory Dix, *The Shape of the Liturgy* (Dacre Press, London, 1945), pp.436-438. This position also enabled Dix to claim that the eventual joining of the word and eucharist liturgies inspired the dropping of the prayers of the faithful at the juncture and replacing them with the intercessions at the end of the eucharistic prayer itself.

[2] Namely, Henri Leclercq, 'Bréviaire,' *Dictionnaire d'Archéologie Chrétienne et la Liturgie* 2:1268; Hélène Pétré, *Éthérie: Journal de voyage* ' "En tes murs, Jérusalem": Histoire et mystére,' in *La Liturgie, son sens, sons esprit, sa méthode: Liturgie et Théologie*, (Bibliotheca Ephemerides Liturgicae Subsidia 27, Rome, 1982), p.244.

[3] See A. A. R. Bastiaensen, *Observations sur la vocubulaire liturgique dans l'Itineraire d'Égérie*, (Latinitas Christianorum Primaeva 17, Nijmegen, 1962), pp.31, 85; Maraval, *Égérie*, pp.246-247n.

[4] Bastiaesen, *Observations*, pp.85-88; Fernand Cabrol *Étude sur la Peregrinatio Sylviae*, (Paris, 1895), pp.54-58; Gingras, *Egeria*, p.222n.

[5] See, Wilkinson, *Egeria's Travels*, p.60; August Bludau, *Die Pilgerreise der Aetheria*, (Paderborn, 1927), p.66; Baldovin, *Urban Character*, pp.58-59.

[6] *Apostolic Constitutions* VII: 26; VIII: 14-15.

[7] On the *missa* structure, see Kavanagh, *Confirmation*, pp.12-14.

B. LITURGY OF THE WORD

We can discern the basic structure of the liturgy of the word at Jerusalem in the fifth century from data in the Armenian Lectionary. Usually the word service follows this pattern:

Psalm (with antiphon)
Reading
Alleluia Psalm (verse)
Gospel
Homily (Homilies)

A similar structure obtained in the contemporary liturgy at Antioch with the exception of another reading before the Gospel and a greeting at the beginning of the liturgy as a whole.[1] It is certainly likely that the hagiopolite liturgy began with a greeting as well, since what is taken for granted is often omitted in liturgical texts. The Georgian Lectionary, actually a compilation of manuscripts witnessing to the state of affairs of the hagiopolite liturgy from the late fifth to the eighth centuries, adds an entrance psalm to the earlier structure.[2] Lectionaries do not provide the prayers of the presider or diaconal litanies and so it is impossible to know, given the state of the evidence, precisely what shape these took during the early part of our period. The ninth century manuscript of the Liturgy of St. James contains a number of prayers of the priest and diaconal litanies, but these may represent a very late stage of development and may not stem from Jerusalem at all.[3]

C. PRE-ANAPHORAL RITES

After the homily (or homilies) the liturgy at Jerusalem continued with litanies for the various groups who were dismissed (catechumens, energumens or the possessed, and penitents) and the prayer of the faithful. As we have noted, Dix

---

[1] See Frans van de Paverd. *Zur Geschichte der Messliturgie in Antiocheia und Konstantinopel gegen Ende des vierten Jahrhunderts*, (Orientalia Christiana Analecta 187, Rome, 1970), pp.82-137.

[2] See Michel Tarchnivvili, *Le grand lectionnaire de l'église de Jérusalem*, (Corpus Christianorum Scriptorum Orientalium 188-189, Louvain, 1959, 2 vols.). For further description, see Helmut Leeb, *Die Gesänge im Gemeindegottesdients von Jerusalem*, (Weiner Beiträge zur Theologie 28, Vienna, 1970) pp.23-33, 43, 62, 87.

[3] B.-Ch. Mercier, *La Liturgie de Saint Jacques*, (Patrologia Orientalis 26, Paris, 1950). The base manuscript is *Ms. Vaticanus Graecus 2282*. The anaphora (eucharistic prayer) is reprinted in A. Hanggi & I. Pahl, eds., *Prex Eucharistica*, (Spicilegium Friburgense 12, Fribourg, 1968), pp.244-261. For an English translation, see Ronald C. D. Jasper and Geoffrey Cuming (eds.), *Prayers of the Eucharist: Early and Reformed*, (Pueblo. Publ. Co., New York, 1987, 3rd ed.), pp.88-89.

For analysis of the manuscript tradition of the Liturgy of St. James in Greek, Syriac, Armenian, Georgian and Ethiopic, see André Tarby, *La Prière Eucharistique de l'Église de Jérusalem*, (Théologie Historique 17, Paris, 1972), pp.28-44.

thought that the intercessions at this point had been dropped and shifted to the anaphora.[1] It is more likely, however, that they remained in this place as in the *Apostolic Constitutions* and that, in a number of liturgies at least, the litanies were added not to the anaphora but to the processional entrance rites.[2]

At this point we can turn to Cyril's description of the eucharist in the fifth mystagogical catechesis. He begins with the washing of the hands of the presider and attendant presbyters a symbolic rather than pragmatic action, intended to connote the purity needed to enter into the eucharist proper. This first mention of the ceremony hints at the shift toward a mystifying piety of awe and trembling that was beginning to characterize Christian liturgical rites in the fourth century.[3] Witnesses after Cyril place this symbolic act of handwashing after the greeting of peace and the presentation of the gifts by the deacons.[4] Although Cyril does not mention this, the hand-washing may have preceded the entrance of the clergy from the nave to the sanctuary, as is suggested by the chants provided to cover this action in the Georgian Lectionary.[5] If this was the case, then the clergy may have presided over the liturgy of the word from a *bema* (platform) in the midst of the nave, as some West Syrian evidence suggests[6], and then entered the sanctuary for the eucharist proper. In support of this we do know from Egeria (45.2) that the bishop's chair can be placed in the midst of the nave; therefore it must have been portable.

If the foregoing scenario stands, then the procession of the gifts would have followed the hand-washing. The Liturgy of St. James is of no help here for the handwashing has disappeared. In any case the Georgian Lectionary also provides chants to accompany the procession of the gifts, among which is the well known Cherubic Hymn, which likely acted as a refrain to the singing of Psalm 24.[7] Since evidence from the fourth century suggests that the procession of the gifts took place in silence, the chants may have developed during the fifth

---

[1] Dix, *Shape of the Liturgy, p.437.*
[2] See John F. Baldovin, 'Kyrie Eleison and the Entrance Rite of the Roman Eucharist,' *Worship* 60, (1986), pp.337-344.
[3] On this subject of mystifying piety, see Alexander Schmemann, *Introduction to Liturgical Theology,* (St. Vladimir's Seminary Press, Crestwood, NY, 1975, 2nd ed.), pp.72-101.
[4] E.g., Theodore, MC IV:42; *Apostolic Constitutions* VIII:11; Dionysius Areogagite, *Ecclesiastical Hierarchy* III:3. For a thorough investigation of this section of the liturgy in the Byzantine tradition, see Robert F. Taft, *The Great Entrance,* (Orientalia Christiana Analecta 200, Rome, 1975), pp.163-164.
[5] See Leeb, *Gesänge.* pp.106-113, where a number of variable texts that accompany the hand-washing are discussed.
[6] See Robert F. Taft, 'Some Notes on the Bema in the East and West-Syrian Traditions,' *Orientalia Christiana Periodica* 34 (1968), p.356.
[7] See Leeb, *Gesänge,* pp.119-124; Taft, *Great Entrance,* pp.69-76.

century, given the tendency of the liturgy to expand at more ceremonial points.[1] Cyril fails to mention a procession with the gifts[2], but it may have taken place. We have already seen in the preceding chapter that he is a selective commentator. The kiss of peace follows in Cyril's exposition of the rite. He emphasizes the symbolic nature of this act; i.e. related to forgiveness and reconciliation. A slight structural shift has taken place here. In Justin Martyr and the *Apostolic Tradition* as well as evidence from Antioch which is contemporary with Cyril, the kiss of peace occurs at the juncture between the common prayers and the procession with the gifts. Slightly later, Theodore of Mopsuestia puts the kiss of peace after the presentation of the gifts and before the handwashing.[3] No doubt, instead of acting as the conclusion of the liturgy of the word, as it had originally, the kiss of peace now prepared directly for the eucharistic prayer and communion, as Cyril makes clear (MC V.3) from his reference to Mt. 5.23 in explaining the gesture.

D. THE EUCHARISTIC PRAYER

The eucharistic prayer at Jerusalem in the late fourth century has given rise to by far the most speculation of any liturgical subject in our study. Contemporary scholarship has been concerned with two main subjects: the structure and content of the prayer described by Cyril in MC V and the sources for the Anaphora of St. James.

The tumultuous fourth century saw the production of a number of eucharistic prayers. Previously it seems that presiders had a good deal of liberty when it came to the content of the prayer as long as they stayed within the confines of certain canonized structures.[4] Concern for orthodox expression and the need to provided presiders who were perhaps less charismatic and less educated with reliable formulae encouraged the development of fixed written texts in the course of the fourth and fifth centuries. No doubt Cyril and his contemporaries witness a period of transition, although the basic lines of the Anaphora of St. James, eventually *the* hagiopolite eucharistic prayer, seem to have been formulated by the early fifth century.[5] We are dealing, then, with a period of rather rapid and effective formulation of prayer styles.

---

[1] On the silent procession, for Antioch, see van de Paverd, *Messliturgie,* pp.243-250; for Syria, Theodore, MC IV:28. On the expansion at ceremonial points, Robert F. Taft, 'How Liturgies Grow: The Evolution of the Byzantine Divine Liturgy,' in *idem., Beyond East and West: Problems in Liturgical Understanding,* (Pastoral Press, Washington, DC, 1984), pp.167-168.

[2] See Justin Martyr, *I -Apology* 65; *Apostolic Tradition* 21; van de Paverd, *Messliturgie,* pp.221-227.

[3] Theodore, MC IV:39-41; for further comment, see Taft, *Great Entrance,* pp.389-392.

[4] See Allan Bouley, *From Freedom to Formula:The Evolution of the Eucharistic Prayer from Oral Improvisation to Written Texts,* (Catholic Univ. of America Press, Washington, DC, 1981), esp. pp.89-158.

[5] See Tarby, *Prière Eucharistique,* pp.45-46.

A schematic outline of the anaphoral structure in both Cyril and James will be helpful:

Cyril (MC V)/James
Dialogue/Dialogue
Praise for Creation/Praise for Creation
Sanctus/Sanctus
Praise for Salvation
Institution Narrative
Anamnesis/Oblation
Epiclesis/Epiclesis
Intercessions/Intercessions
Doxology/Amen.

James represents what has come to be called the West Syrian or Antiochene structure logical and smooth in its development of themes. In this it is similar to the Anaphoras of Basil (both Alexandrian and Byzantine), John Chrysostom, the Twelve Apostles, and Book VIII of the Apostolic Constitutions among others.[1] The earliest example of this structure has now been determined to stem from *ca.* 300, a Coptic translation of a Greek original, usually called Alexandrian Basil to distinguish it from the theologically reworked recension of the later fourth century, known as Byzantine Basil and still used several times a year in Byzantine churches.[2]

Speculation with regard to the eucharistic prayer alluded to by Cyril centres on whether or not it contained an institution narrative. The institution narrative is mentioned in MC IV but not in the course of the description of the eucharistic prayer. Cutrone argues that Cyril has intentionally commented on the institution narrative in a distinct lecture precisely because the hagiopolite prayer did not contain the narrative. Since, he claims, Cyril has explained baptism by the method of *eikonmimesis*, which we have seen in the preceding chapter, he also wishes to apply the same scheme to the eucharist. And so, since the eucharistic prayer his listeners are familiar with contains no such narrative, MC IV provides the needed commentary as to how the eucharist effects union with Christ. Cutrone's thesis rests upon Cyril's use of *eita* (next) when he is proceeding point by point as compared with *meta tauta* (after this) when he clearly omits some material.[3]

Alternative theories argue that the eucharistic prayer described by Cyril did indeed contain an institution narrative. For example, when citing the narrative in

---

[1] See Hanggi/Pahl, *Prex Eucharistique*, pp.204-373.

[2] For further description, see John Fenwick, *Fourth Century Anaphoral Construction Techniques*, (Grove Liturgical Study 45, Bramcote, Notts., 1986), pp.6-10; Jasper/Cuming, *Prayers of the Eucharist*, pp.67-69, 114-115.

[3] Emmanuel J. Cutrone, 'Cyril's Mystagogical Catecheses and the Evolution of the Jerusalem Anaphora,' *Orientalia Christiana Periodica* 44 (1978), pp.52-64. Fenwick (*Anaphoral Construction*, pp.13-15) finds Cutrone's argument persuasive.

MC IV Cyril claims to be quoting St. Paul (I Cor. 11.23), the passage which the neophytes have just heard. The words of institution he cites, however, are not taken directly from Paul but are clearly a conflation of the Pauline and Matthean accounts.[1] Thus Cyril was apparently well acquainted with a *liturgical* institution narrative. Another reason for the omission of the narrative in MC V may have been related to the silent recitation of certain parts of the eucharistic prayer by the end of the fourth century.[2] This could account for Cyril passing over the words of institution when describing the prayer. Finally, immediately after speaking of the epiclesis, Cyril says:

'Then, after the spiritual sacrifice is perfected, the bloodless service upon that sacrifice of propitiation, we entreat God for the common peace of the church ...' (MC V.8)

On the basis of an analogous comment in the writing of John Chrysostom, Cuming interpreted the 'perfecting' of the sacrifice to mean the institution narrative. This would suggest that Cyril was describing a eucharistic prayer akin to the Egyptian tradition of Serapion, the Deir Balyzeh Papyrus, the Louvain Coptic Papyrus, and later the Anaphora of St. Mark, where the epiclesis precedes the institution narrative.[3]

In my opinion the arguments that propose an institution narrative in Cyril's eucharistic prayer have more weight. Taken singly none is probative, but considered together they are more persuasive than arguments for its absence. As we saw when dealing with initiation, Cyril did not feel constrained to comment on every element in the rites. In addition he may have failed to speak of the institution narrative in MC *because* he had already singled it out for explanation in the preceding lecture. If Cuming was correct about the Egyptian origin of Cyril's prayer, then very shortly after Cyril Jerusalem must have adopted the West Syrian form of anaphora, in which the epiclesis followed upon the institution narrative, anamnesis and oblation.[4]

---

[1] As noted, e.g., in Massey H. Shepherd, 'Eusebius and the Liturgy of Saint James,' *Yearbook of Liturgical Studies* 4 (1963), pp.121-123; and Georg Kretschmar, 'Abendmahlsfeier,' *Theologische Reäl-Encyclopädie* I (Berlin, 1977), p.254.

[2] See Kretschmar, 'Frühe Geschichte,' p.254.

[3] Geoffrey J. Cuming, 'Egyptian Elements in the Jerusalem Liturgy,' *Journal of Theological Studies*, n.s. 23 (1971), pp.118-119.

[4] Indeed Fenwick has argued (*Anaphoral Construction*, pp.26-30, 33-34) that James is the result of a conflation of Alexandrian Basil with material from Cyril. The influence of the Basil Anaphora may have been determinative in changing the structure of the hagiopolite eucharistic prayer. For my hypothesis to be correct I would have to challenge Fenwick's dating of the conflation at 368-370, since the Mystagogical Catecheses of Cyril were most probably delivered some ten to fifteen years later. A connection between Basil and James had originally been suggested by Hans Lietzmann, *Mass and Lord's Supper*, (ET, E. J. Brill, Leiden, 1973-1979), pp.27, 44, 116 and by Dix, *Shape of the Liturgy*, p.204.

One other aspect of the eucharistic prayer at Jerusalem needs to be addressed, namely the epiclesis. Although Cyril and the Anaphora of James by no means represent the earliest instance of an epiclesis in a eucharistic prayer, they do signal an important change in its function. In Cyril (MC V.7; see MC IV.2) the Holy Spirit is called down to change (*metaballein*) the elements of bread and wine into the body and blood of Christ. The explicit notion of change is innovative with regard to the epiclesis. Together with another innovative verb, *poiein* (to make) Cyril signals a shift from previous tradition; i.e. we can now begin to pinpoint a 'moment of consecration.'[1] Explicit focus on such a moment may not have been Cyril's intent, but the wording of the prayer and Cyril's commentary did inspire later Eastern tradition to isolate the epiclesis as the moment of transformation in much the same way the Western tradition concentrated on the words of institution. The Anaphora of James adopts the same 'consecratory' vocabulary in its epiclesis by the use of the verb 'to make.'

In James the epiclesis itself is a rather complex construction. In the Greek recension we find a two-fold request that the Holy Spirit be sent down upon the communicants and the gifts. The Syriac text, which probably represents an earlier form[2], reveals a simpler wording. As Spinks has shown, the first and earlier verb employed was *exapostellein* (to send forth), which may have been peculiar to hagopolite tradition. A later stratum, represented in the Greek text, employs a characteristically Antiochene verb *katapempein* (to send down).[3] Thus we may have another indication that hagiopolite liturgical tradition was formed from many sources, not merely that of the West Syrian tradition.

E. COMMUNION AND DISMISSAL

At the end of his commentary on the eucharistic prayer Cyril turns to the Lord's Prayer (MC V.11). In this earliest mention of the Lord's Prayer in a eucharistic context the phrase 'give us this day our daily (supersubstantial) bread' is interpreted in terms of holy communion.[4]

Cyril passes over the fraction rite in silence; it may well have taken place between the anaphora itself and the Lord's Prayer as in the contemporary eucharistic rite at Antioch.[5] In any case the fraction rite follows the Lord's Prayer

---

[1] See Dix, *Shape of the Liturgy*, pp.277-280.
[2] For the Syriac recension, see O. Heiming, *Anaphora Syriaca sancti Jacobi fratris Domini*, (Anaphorae Syriacae II:2, Rome, 1953), pp.105-179. In Latin translation this version can be found in Hanggi/Pahl, *Prex Eucharistica*, pp.269-275. For the hypothetical reconstruction of the original Greek form of the prayer, see Tarby, *Prière Eucharistique*, pp.45-70.
[3] Nryan Spinks, 'The Consecratory Epiclesis in the Anaphora of St. James,' *Studia Liturgica* II (1976), pp.31-33. On the other hand the Syriac recension represents an elaboration on the (original) Greek in terms of the effects of consecration. see *ibid.*, p.35.
[4] See Piédagnel, *Cyrille*, p.161n.
[5] See van de Paverd, *Messliturgie*, pp.369-371.
[6] Mercier, *Litrugie de S. Jacques*, pp.228-230.

in the Liturgy of St. James.[6] Next comes the invitation to communion. 'Holy things to the holy,' with the response. 'One is Holy, One is the Lord, Jesus Christ' (MC V.19). We find the same invitation in the *Apostolic Constitutions* and Theodore of Mopsuestia.[1] In both of these sources, however, the response is more elaborate. Cyril may be providing a resume of the response, as Piédagnel suggests[2], but it is also possible that the originally brief response was expanded in *Apostolic Constitutions*, the liturgy described by Theodore, and subsequently the Liturgy of St. James.[3]

The cantor then invites the people to communion with the psalm verse. 'Taste and see that the Lord is good (Ps. 34.8; MC V.20). The same verse is cited in James. It is likely that not simply this one verse but rather that the entire psalm was sung responsorially while the people communicated and that the verse acted as a refrain.[4] Cyril seems not so much interested in describing what was sung as with the attitude of the communicants, who are to make of their extended palms a throne for God and to touch the consecrated bread to their eyes before consuming it (MC V.21). Again, with the cup, after responding 'Amen' to words of institution (which are not cited) the communicant is to touch the moisture on the lips to the brow and other senses. Of course Cyril has already explained the identification with Christ's body and blood in MC IV.3, where he uses the phrase *en typo* ('in a figure') but clearly intends to communicate a real participation as he did with similar language in the second and third mystagogies. The eucharistic rite concludes with a postcommunion prayer and presumably a dismissal. Cyril says nothing about a procession to the Anastasis, but that may have simply been outside of the purview of his lectures.

We have found that the eucharistic liturgy at Jerusalem assumed its classic shape by the late fourth century and was subsequently expanded at the action-points in a manner similar to other Eastern and Western liturgies. Aspects mentioned by Cyril for the first time (the Lord's Prayer, handwashing, invitation to communion) were probably not so much hagiopolite innovations as examples of a common development in the ceremonial and structure of the eucharist everywhere in the fourth century. But Jerusalem, especially as we have seen with regard to the eucharistic prayer, acted as a crossroads for a number of liturgical traditions.

---

[1] *Apostolic Constitutions,* VIII:13; Theodore, MC V:23.
[2] Piédagnel, *Cyrille,* p.169.
[3] Mercier, *Liturgie de S. Jacques,* p.232.
[4] See Leeb, *Gesänge,* pp.128-133; also Thomas H. Schattauer, 'The Koinonicon of the Byzantine Liturgy: An Historical Study,' *Orientalia Christiana Periodica* 49 (1983), pp.91-129.

4. The Daily Office

Among all of the topics dealt with in liturgical studies probably none is more difficult and complex than the origins and development of the daily office or liturgy of the hours. We are fortunate that for the Jerusalem church we have a thorough and detailed description of how the various offices of the day were carried out. That description comes to us from Egeria's pilgrimage diary.

Before we deal with Egeria's description, however, we should clarify a distinction that is commonly made today about the office: the distinction between Cathedral and Monastic prayer. The first real evidence that we possess for how the daily offices were actually carried out comes to us from the fourth century.[1] The Monastic form of the office in Egypt and Syria stressed contemplation and the form of psalmody consisted mainly in the ascetics' listening to a solo reader. There was very little ritual associated with this prayer which encouraged the monks to pray always (I Thess.5.5). We call this style of office Monastic. Around the same time as the development of this Monastic form, we find the liturgy of the hours being celebrated in major churches. This office was characterized not so much by contemplation as by communal praise and intercession, ritual like the lighting of lamps and use of incense, and the presence of official ecclesiastical figures, especially the bishop. That is why this form of the office is called Cathedral prayer it was presided over by the bishop or his representative. Today this popular form of the office would be called parochial prayer. In addition to the focus on ritualization and communal praise and intercession, the Cathedral form of the office was also characterized by the use of psalms appropriate to the particular time of day that the office was being celebrated as we shall see below.

As we shall see the two traditions of Monastic and Cathedral office are represented in the liturgy described by Egeria. She recounts five daily offices (a vigil, morning prayer, prayer at the sixth and ninth hour, and evening prayer), a vigil that is held only on Sundays, and a service that is held only in Lent (prayer at the third hour).[2]

The first office that Egeria recounts is monastic in nature a daily vigil held, as are most of the daily offices, in the Anastasis. The vigil begins before cockcrow and is attended mainly by urban monks and nuns (*monazontes* and *parthenae*) and by some layfolk. The office consists of hymns, responsorial psalms and

---

[1] See Robert F. Taft, *The Liturgy of the Hours in East and West* (Sollegeville, MN, 1986), 31ff.

[2] The terminology of the office like its structures can be confusing. The vigil is sometimes called Matins; morning prayer has been called both Matins and Lauds. Egeria's name for Lauds is *matutini ymni* (24:2). I will retain Egeria's terminology as much as possible. The services at the third, sixth, and ninth hours were held at what we should call 9 a.m., noon, and 3 p.m. However, we should note that in this pre-clock culture the amount of time in the hours of the day depended on the amount of daylight at the particular time of the year.

antiphons, all of which seem to be interchangeable terms for our pilgrim.[1] Presbyters and deacons are present at this office on a rotating schedule to say the prayers that come after each of the hymns and psalms.[2] The office ends before dawn. What makes this vigil monastic in nature is the absence of the bishop. In addition Egeria does not inform us as to the content of the hymns and psalms, but since she does not add her usual comment on their appropriateness to the day and place, we may presume that the ascetics prayed the psalms one after the other without regard to whether they fit the hour of the day.

The next service presents us with a somewhat different picture of the office. *Matutini ymni* (Morning Prayer) begins at dawn and like the vigil is held at the Anastasis.It is cathedral in nature. Egeria does not inform us as to precisely what was sung at this office, but it is likely that Ps.63, *the* morning psalm as well as other psalms and hymns were employed.[3] The bishop and clergy arrive after the beginning of the service and the bishop enters the chancel of the edicule covering the cave of the resurrection to say the Prayer for All, which seems to have been a general prayer of intercession. In the course of that prayer Egeria notes that he mentions the names of individuals he wishes to pray for. Then he blesses the catechumens, says another prayer and blesses the faithful. After the blessings he comes out of the chancel and everyone comes to his hand for an individual blessing.[4] Thus the dismissal takes place when it is already daylight. Note that the eucharist is not celebrated on a daily basis. Egeria informs us that it takes place on Sundays and Wednesdays and Fridays outside of Lent. In all probability it was also celebrated on Saturdays since this is a day when there is no fasting. (27.1) At the sixth hour and again at the ninth hour the people assemble at the Anastasis with the bishop again for services that include psalms and antiphons. As with Morning Prayer the bishop is sent for only after the psalms and antiphons have begun. Once again he enters the chancel of the edicule over the cave and says a prayer and blessing. (24.3) The people come to his hand as at Morning Prayer. . During Lent an extra hour is added the third hour and it conforms to the structure we have seen for sext and none. (27.4) The service at the

---

[1] See Wilkinson, *Egeria's Travels,* 55.

[2] The saying of prayers between psalms seems to have been a characteristic of vigils as opposed to other early liturgical hours; see Paul F. Bradshaw, *Daily Prayer in the Early Church* (Alcuin/SPCK, London, 1981), pp.85, 94ff.

[3] This was the morning psalm at Antioch, *Apostolic Constitutions* II:59. The morning office at Jerusalem may well have included the hymn *Gloria in Excelsis* as well, see Taft, *Liturgy of the Hours,* pp.44-47, 55-56.

[4] It is difficult to know precisely what the phrase 'to come to the hand' means. Recently Kavanagh (*Confirmation*) has argued at some length that it means an imposition of hands. Wilkinson (*Egeria's Travels,* p.123) translates the phrase as to kiss the hand of the bishop. It seems to me that the phrase probably means kissing the bishop's hand as in the popular Mediterranean custom exemplified by the Italian baciamo la mano.

One must agree, however, with Kavanagh that the missa must have taken a considerable amount of time, even if every single person did not have the opportunity to get an individual blessing from the bishop.

tenth hour (around four in the afternoon) reveals not only the nature of the fourth century Cathedral office but also the genius of the Jerusalem liturgy. The people assemble as usual at the Anastasis. Lamps and candles are lit even though it is daylight and Egeria notes that there is considerable light (*lucem infinitum*). The light comes from a lamp burning night and day inside the edicule over the cave, no doubt to symbolize Christ as the true source of light. (24.5) The service itself is called *licinicon* in Greek, which Egeria translates as *Lucernare*. The bishop is sent for, enters with the clergy and sits at his throne. Meanwhile the *Lucernare* psalms and antiphons continue. These most probably included the universal evening psalm in the East Psalm 141 as well as the hymn, *Phos hilaron* (O Gladsome Light) in addition to other psalm. This final part of the daily *Lucernare* is what is most characteristic of the Jerusalem daily office. The office itself takes advantage not only of the site of Christ's resurrection but of the other sacred spots within the Golgotha precinct. That this practice made a profound impression on visitors to Jerusalem is witnessed by the fact that the Easter vespers at Rome and Milan in later centuries concluded with a procession to a chapel of the Cross located in the baptistery.

A final comment with regard to readings from Scripture. There were none in the daily office as the observant reader has by now observed. In fact none of the early Cathedral offices contained readings from Scripture, with the exception of the last element we are about to treat. As Zerfass has pointed out readings came into the office by way of the commemorative liturgical services that were held at holy places and on special days.[1] This is witnessed abundantly by both Egeria and the subsequent Armenian Lectionary.

The Jerusalem office which has most affected subsequent liturgies is the Sunday cathedral vigil.[2] It will be readily apparent that this vigil differs significantly from the daily monastic vigil described above. Egeria informs us that on Sunday a large crowd gathers before cockcrow in the *Ad Crucem* atrium; i.e. between the Martyrium and the Anastasis. (24.8) They sing hymns and psalms while waiting for the doors of the Anastasis to be opened and, presbyters and deacons are present to say prayers between them. At cockcrow the bishop himself enters and goes immediately to the cave (edicule). The Anastasis has already been lit with lamps. All the people come in and three psalms are said in responsorial fashion with prayers between led respectively by a presbyter, a deacon, and another member of the clergy.[3] The psalmody is followed by the intercessory Prayer for All and by an incensation of the entire Anastasis. The bishop then goes inside the chancel of the edicule and reads the gospel of the resurrection (24.10), that is the entire passion and resurrection narrative, for Egeria mentions that all the people

---

[1] Rolf Zerfass, *Die Schriftlesung im Kathedraloffizium Jerusalems,* = LQF 48, (Münster, 1968), pp.1-15.

[2] For a full treatment of this service, see J. Mateos, 'La vigile cathédrale chez Égérie' in OCP 27 (1961), pp.281-312.

[3] Gingras, *Egeria*, p.219, n.289, thinks that these are the traditional lauds psalms (Pss.148-150), but we do not possess enough evidence to make this affirmation.

groan at the beginning of the reading.[1] This gospel reading is the sentre of the service and shows the influence of the stational services that contained readings—services that may well have been created for the pilgrims to the holy city.[2]

After the reading of the gospel the bishop emerges from the chancel and all go in procession to the *Ad Crucem* atrium where they have a final psalm, a prayer, the blessing, and all come to the bishop's hand. The bishop then retires to his residence while the monks and layfolk that wish stay on to continue singing psalms and saying prayers until dawn. This last service is most likely the equivalent of the daily monastic vigil.

CONCLUSION
What then have we learned from this brief survey of daily prayer in the Jerusalem church? Once again we have seen that hagiopolite liturgy was basically similar to other major centers in the late fourth/early fifth centuries. At the same time Jerusalem added two aspects to the liturgy of the hours that were to have a significant impact on the development of liturgical prayer in general. Both of these elements were related to the specific character of hagiopolite liturgical life and piety.

In the first place Jerusalem is the first witness to the Cathedral Vigil on Sunday morning, a practice which is continued today in the Byzantine office. It is in this vigil that we note the addition of a reading from Scripture (the Gospel of Christ's Passion and Resurrection) for the first time. Probably derived from the Jerusalem pilgrim practice of reading selections from Scripture at the sacred sites, this liturgical element soon found its way into other Cathedral offices. It was not native to the Cathedral tradition, which was originally orientated to praise and intercession. This might raise questions today about the nature and necessity of Scripture reading in the daily office—certainly an almost heretical suggestion after the Reformation insistence on such reading.

The second peculiarity of the hagiopolite office is its stational character. The processions that ended the Cathedral Vigil, Morning Prayer and Lucernare ensured that the praying community touched base at each of the major shrines within the Holy Sepulchre complex several times each day. Though this practice had its imitators in several other churches (especially in the Roman Easter Sunday Vespers) it is clear that its inspiration was the desire to venerate the holy sites themselves. Such stational practice is highlighted by the Jerusalem observance of the liturgical calendar, which is the subject of our final chapter.

---

[1] Mateos, 'Vigile cathédrale', p.291, notes that this reading demonstrates the close theological connection between the passion and resurrection in Jerusalem at this time.

[2] See Zerfass, *Schriftlesung*, pp.15-19. For this reading in the later Armenian Rite, see C. Renoux, 'Les lectures quadragésimales du rite arménien' REA 5 (1968), pp.241-243; for other rites, Mateos, 'Vigile cathédrale', pp.296-310.

5. The Liturgical Year

A. INTRODUCTION

The most significant contribution of the liturgy in Jerusalem on both East and West has been its influence on the Christian calendar. In fact the importance of Jerusalem led Gregory Dix to see in its fourth century calendar the origins of an entirely new Christian concept of time, namely a shift from eschatology to historicization.[1] Quite recently this notion has received considerable nuance. Although the Jerusalem liturgy may have been responsible for the spread and popularity of a number of feasts, it did not represent a radical shift in the Christian notion of time nor was it necessarily the origin of a number of celebrations which had been attributed to it.[2] Moreover, it is important to note that the primitive stratum of hagiopolite practice can be discerned in the use of its 'gospel of choice', namely Matthew. Talley has shown that services which employ the other three gospels have a tendency to be later developments.[3]

What made the hagiopolite calendar of feasts distinctive? Quite simply it was the (now Christian) possession of holy sites associated with events in the life of Christ, the lives of the saints and the Hebrew Scriptures which provided the impetus for developing feasts, which could then be universalized.[4] As we shall see, this general principle does not account for every development in the calendar at Jerusalem, but does provide a starting point for the development of what has come to be called the liturgical year. The key to understanding the relation of place to feast in the Jerusalem liturgy is a phenomenon called stational liturgy, in which the place of liturgical celebration varied according to the feast. The stational system at Jerusalem can be distinguished from that at Rome and Constantinople, for example, in that it depended in large part on possession of sites related to the life of Christ.[5]

---

[1] Gregory Dix, *The Shape of the Liturgy* (Dacre Press, London, 1945), pp.303-319.

[2] See Talley, *Origins*, pp.42-47, 176-183; Robert Taft, 'Historicism Revisited' in *idem.*, *Beyond East and West: Problems in Liturgical Understanding* (Pastoral Press, Washington, DC, 1984), pp.23-26; Baldovin, *Urban Character*, pp.102-104.

[3] Talley, *Origins*, p.44.

[4] See Baldovin, *Urban Character*, pp.83-87; Jonathan Z. Smith, *To Take Place: Toward Theory in Ritual*, (Univ. of Chicago Press, Chicago, 1987), pp.74-95. Some sites, of course, had been associated with Christian memory if not liturgical celebration, long before the fourth century. With particular relation to the Mount of Olives, for example, see Georg Kretschmar, 'Festkalendar und Memorialstätten Jerusalems' *Zeitschrift des Deutschen Palästina-Vereins* 87 (1971), pp.167-205.

[5] See Baldovin, *Urban Character*, pp.231-234.

In outlining the liturgical year at Jerusalem we shall follow the sequence described by Egeria and confirmed by the Armenian and Georgian Lectionaries; i.e. beginning with the celebration of the Incarnation (Epiphany and/or Christmas) rather than the most important feast of the year the Easter Triduum. In fact, as Talley has shown, the celebration of the Incarnation marked the beginning of the annual liturgical cycle in all the major liturgical traditions.[1]

B. EPIPHANY AND RELATED FEASTS

The origin of the feast of the Epiphany is an enormously complex and highly debated matter. Despite the fact that it may well lie in a heterodox Christian celebration of the Baptism of Christ[2], the original celebration of Epiphany at Jerusalem seems to have focussed exclusively on the nativity, at least as far as the evidence of Egeria and the Armenian Lectionary is concerned.[3] Thus Jerusalem stands alone among the Eastern traditions of the fifth century in not associating the Epiphany with the baptism of Christ. It seems that the Jerusalem church may have adopted the Western Nativity feast (the December 25th Christmas) for a brief period in the midfifth century (after the Council of Ephesus), but it was not until the late sixth century (as witnessed by the Georgian Lectionary) that this latter feast was definitively inserted into the hagiopolite calendar.

Why was Jerusalem so tardy in accepting the Western Christmas date? Possibly because the association between January 6 and the place of the Nativity was so strong. Or perhaps it had to do more with theological factors like the Monophysite resistance to splitting the feasts of the Incarnation into one which would emphasis the human nature of Christ (Christmas) and another which stressed his divine manifestation (Epiphany).[4]

According to the evidence of the pilgrimage diary of Egeria and the compilation of manuscripts referred to as the old Armenian Lectionary the Epiphany celebration in late fourth/early fifth century Jerusalem consisted of the following elements: a procession from Jerusalem to Bethlehem with a brief stational service along the way at 'The Place of the Shepherds,' a vigil at the Bethlehem basilica on the night between January 5 and 6, ending with a celebration of the eucharist, a procession back to Jerusalem on the morning of January 6 with morning prayer and another eucharist at the Golgotha Martyrium, and an octave with daily celebration of the eucharist at the stations shown in the table overleaf.

---

[1] Talley, *Origins*, pp.129-134.
[2] See Garielle Winkler, 'Epiphany', and also Talley, *Origins*, pp.103-129.
[3] On this question, see Athanase Renoux, 'L'Epiphanie à Jérusalem au IVme et au Vme siècle' in *Revue des Etudes Arméniennes* 2 (1965), pp.343-359.
[4] For this argument, see Michel van Esbroeck, 'La lettre de l'empereur Justinien et la Nöel en 561' in *Analecta Bollandina* 86 (1968), pp.351-371.

Epiphany Octave	Egeria	Armenian Lectionary
Jan. 6	Martyrium	Martyrium
Jan. 7	Martyrium	St. Stephen's
Jan. 8	Martyrium	Martyrium (Sunday)
Jan. 9	leona	Sion
Jan. 10	Lazarium	Eleona
Jan. 11	Sion	Lazarium
Jan. 12	Anastasis	Martyrium
Jan. 13	Ad Crucem	Anastasis

The commemoration of the presentation of Jesus in the Temple, celebrated on the fortieth day after Epiphany (February 14), was related to this major feast. Of course, the date of the celebration was shifted to February 2 after Jerusalem adopted the Western Nativity date (December 25). The Anastasis, considered the new Temple, served as the station for the service.

A further stage in the development of the Jerusalem calendar is represented by the Georgian Lectionary, which witnesses a December 25 Nativity celebration as well as a January 6 Epiphany. Thus the Georgian Lectionary contains a vigil as well as an octave for each of these feasts. A comparative reading of the various stages revealed by Egeria, the Armenian Lectionary, and theGeorgian Lectionary provides a great deal of information as to the development of the hagiopolite liturgical calendar. I will mention only a few.

First, the vigil reported in the Armenian Lectionary consists of eleven readings and a canticle (Daniel 3.35-90), all from the Old Testament, and is most probably modelled on the Paschal Vigil. Three of the readings and the canticle (except for the poetic refrain) repeat selections found in the Paschal Vigil.[1] The remaining readings, taken mainly from Isaiah, emphasize the incarnational focus of the feast. In the later stage, represented by the Georgian Lectionary, the Epiphany readings of the Armenian Lectionary are transferred to the Christmas vigil, and new readings, related to the Baptism of the Lord, have been adopted for the Epiphany vigil. Second, the Armenian Lectionary witnesses to two eucharistic celebrations, the Georgian Lectionary to three.But the eucharist which concludes the vigil in the Armenian Lectionary has for a gospel selection Matthew 2.1-12 (the visit of the Magi)—surely an odd reading for a nativity feast? Only later, at the morning eucharist, does one find the Matthean account of the nativity of Christ (Mt 1.18-23). Why this confusing arrangement of readings? Here the arrangement of the liturgical stations may shed some light. As one can observe in the chart printed above, on January 7 the Armenian Lectionary contains a station which is absent from Egeria's list, namely St. Stephen's, which was almost certainly added after the discovery of the relics of Stephen in 415.[2] This new arrangement inspired the selection of a gospel more appropriate to the

---

[1] For a comparative table of the vigil readings in the Armenian and Georgian Lectionaries, see Rolf Zerfass, *Die Schriftlesung im Kathedraloffizium Jerusalems* (Liturgiewissenschaftliche Quellen und Forschungen 48, Müster, 1968), pp.100-101.

[2] See Renoux, *Codex Jerusalem Arménien*, pp.59-64, 216n.

place (the diaconicon of Sion) and the commemoration (Stephen), namely John 12.24-26. It is likely that this latter pericope replaced the reading of Mt 2.12, which was then shifted to the vigil service and that Mt 1.18-23 had originally been read both at the vigil and the morning eucharist with the story of the Magi read on the second day of the octave. Thus from a rather minute detail one can make a number of observations about the development of Jerusalem's liturgical calendar. that the cult of St. Stephen was popular enough to inspire a shift in the traditional stational arrangement, that the morning eucharist at Jerusalem and not the one at the vigil represents the most primitive celebration of the feast for this church, since it retained the original gospel reading, that the readings tended to be chosen more for their association with place than thematic development, and finally that the most primitive stratum of the Jerusalem liturgy followed a course reading of Matthew's Gospel.[1]

Third, one other oddity of the Epiphany octave readings may be mentioned. In the Armenian Lectionary for January 11 the gospel selection is John 11.1-46. Obviously the story of the raising of Lazarus, like the January 7 selection from John 12, does not fit with the rest of the readings of the octave, all relating aspects of the infancy narratives. Once again the arrangement of the stations provides the clue to solving an anomaly. The station at the Lazarium at Bethany (employed on January 10 in Egeria) was apparently more significant than festal themes in determining the reading for the day.

From these few observations one can begin to understand that the development of a liturgical calendar, and especially that of Jerusalem, was strongly related to the particular traditions of a place. One consequence of the hagiopolite arrangement and its peculiarities may have been the adoption of the Magi gospel for Epiphany in the Roman liturgy.

C. LENT

The nature and duration of the Lenten observance at Jerusalem has been the object of a great deal of speculation. In what follows we can attempt only to outline some of the important issues.

1. *Duration*

How long did Lent last in Jerusalem in the fourth and fifth centuries? The answer to this question cannot be a simple one since the sources reveal 1) a distinction between the Lenten fast and Holy (Great) Week and 2) a (unique) eight-week period mentioned by Egeria. The most penetrating analysis of this question has been performed by M.F. Lages, whose argument we shall summarize briefly. Three distinct *ordines* (daily readings, catechetical readings, and Holy Week readings) can be discerned in the Lenten section of the Armenian Lectionary. Lages argues that each represents an originally separate *libellus* (small

---

[1] For further argument on this last point, see Talley, *Origins*, p.44.

book for the order of service).[1] By means of a structural analysis of the various orders of service found within the Lenten daily readings, he reasons that before the middle of the fourth century Jerusalem, like Rome, knew a three-week Lent preceding Easter, and that the nineteen catechetical lectures were given during these weeks. A six-week fast, distinct from Holy Week, was introduced some time during the second half of the fourth century. Egeria's eight-week fast (seven weeks plus Holy Week) represents a (shortlived) attempt to provide forty fast days.[2] A somewhat different approach has been taken by Talley, who argues that the Jerusalem Lent is a conflation of two distinct *types* of fast. the fast of Holy Week and a forty-day fast in imitation of the fast of Jesus, which originally followed Epiphany in the Alexandrian church. Space does not permit us to review the details of Talley's argument. Suffice it to say that his reconstruction explains the two-day festal period (Lazarus Saturday and Palm Sunday) that separates the Lenten fast proper from Holy Week.[3] Sometime during the fourth century the following may well have happened: an Alexandrian forty-day fast in imitation of Jesus' forty days in the desert (which is described by the Synoptics immediately after his baptism and which was concluded with Christian initiation) was added (via Constantinople?) to the pre-paschal fast observed at Jerusalem and elsewhere. This argument does not necessarily preclude an original three-week Lenten fast at Jerusalem; it also suggests that the celebration of Lazarus Saturday and Palm Sunday (albeit without the topographical peculiarities) may not have been native to Jerusalem.

2.Content and Structure

In early fifth century Jerusalem Lent consisted of six weeks of fasting, begun on a Monday and a final week's fast (Holy Week) separated from the former by Lazarus Saturday and Palm Sunday. Egeria informs us of the nature of fasting during this period as well as the extra daily prayer at the third hour (terce), and a procession on Fridays after vespers from Sion to the Anastasis where an all-night vigil is held. In addition she mentions that on Wednesdays and Fridays a service is held at Sion. This service does not consist of the eucharist during Lent, since (as is common in the Christian East) the eucharist is not held on fast days (27.1; 29.1). The Armenian Lectionary confirms the data provided by Egeria. It supplies readings (all from the Old Testament) for the Wednesdays and Fridays of Lent. The second week represents an exception in that there are readings given for Monday, Tuesday and Thursday (at the Anastasis, not Sion) as well.[4] Perhaps the second week was originally the first week of Lent. No readings are mentioned

---

[1] Mario-Ferreira Lages, 'Étapes de l'Evolution du Carême à Jérusalem avant le Vme siècle: essai d'analyse structurale' in *Revue des Études Armeniénnes* n.s., (1969), pp.72-76.
[2] For a different attempt to explain Egeria's eight weeks, as well as a competent review of the literature, see Johnson.
[3] See Talley, *Origins*, pp.168-222.
[4] On the various structures and the content of the readings, see Lages, 'Évolution du Carême,' pp.76-96.

for Saturdays and Sundays in the Armenian Lectionary. I have already argued that Cyril's catechetical lectures allow one to speculate that what eventually became the Byzantine lectionary (reading Hebrews and Mark on these days) was already the practice in fourth century Jerusalem. Why no mention of these readings in the Armenian Lectionary? Perhaps another set of Saturday/Sunday readings was already employed in Armenia at the time of the compilation of this lectionary and only those aspects of hagiopolite practice that were new were identified. Lages' suggestion that the Lenten elements of the Armenian Lectionary were originally *libelli* would support this hypothesis. In any case the Georgian Lectionary has a completely different set of readings for Saturdays and Sundays.

3. *Lazarus Saturday/Palm Sunday*
We have already seen that these two days have a non-hagiopolite origin according to Talley. On the Saturday before Holy Week the Jerusalem community processed to Bethany, a few kilometres from Jerusalem over the Mount of Olives. On the way they held a brief prayer service with a reading from John's Gospel about Jesus meeting Mary (Jn.11.29; Egeria 29.4). This was followed by another prayer service at the Lazarium in Bethany, which consisted of a reading of the gospel of the raising of Lazarus and a solemn announcement of the feast of Easter (Egeria 29.5-6).[1] Oddly enough the Armenian Lectionary indicates that the gospel reading was John 11.55-12.11. Perhaps in view of the length of the coming Holy Week services the gospel of the raising of Lazarus was dropped, since it was also read during the Epiphany octave at the station at the Lazarium. The next day included a long afternoon prayer-service and procession down the Mount of Olives to the city, as well as the usual eucharist in the morning. By the time of the Georgian-Lectionary this long service and procession had been shifted to the morning before the eucharist.[2] Although Talley may be correct in suggesting that Palm Sunday itself did not originate in Jerusalem, certainly the procession which was to have so much influence in other churches did stem from that church's liturgical practice.

D. EASTER
No doubt the most significant aspect of the Jerusalem liturgical practice, especially during the Triduum (Maundy Thursday, Good Friday, the Paschal Vigil) and the Easter Season was its stational character. Various sites in and around Jerusalem were employed for the many services held during this period. The stations themselves shaped the liturgical celebration considerably.

---

[1] Although Talley (*Origins*, p.178) claims that Egeria does not mention that the raising of Lazarus was the reading, it seems clear enough from the text, especially since the announcement of Easter included Jn.11.55-12.11, which later became the Armenian Lectionary's sole text.
[2] *Georgian Lectionary*, nos. 576-600.

1. Maundy Thursday

Two major services were held on this day. 1) the eucharist during the afternoon at the Martyrium, and 2) an all-night vigil on the Mount of Olives followed by a solemn procession back to the city by daybreak.

The eucharist itself seems to have commemorated the Last Supper of Jesus. Although Egeria (35.1) says nothing about a thematic character to this celebration, she does mention that a second celebration followed immediately upon the first. The second took place in a small chapel next to Golgotha, called *Post Crucem* (Behind the Cross). The Armenian Lectionary provides readings for the celebration on this day; they relate the institution of the eucharist. In the Armenian Lectionary, however, a third celebration is held at Sion, now (in the fifth century) identified as the site of the Last Supper.[1] Moreover the second celebration has been shifted to the atrium 'Before the Cross', a larger space. Perhaps the reason for the second eucharist at the Golgotha complex was an overflow of crowds on this day.[2] The Georgian Lectionary adds a solemn service of reconciliation of penitents on the morning of Maundy Thursday as well as a washing of the feet after the gospel at the eucharist. There is no mention of a second or third eucharist. The station is the Martyrium.

The all-night vigil at the Eleona, then the Imbomon and then (with a procession to Gethsemane) down the Mount of Olives had as its centrepiece a reading of the entire Last Supper discourse from the Gospel of John (Jn. 13.16-18.1).[3] The various manuscripts of the Armenian Lectionary manifest a tendency to co-ordinate the sites for reading the successive gospel passages ever more closely with events in the Gospel.

2. Good Friday

Three services comprised the observance of Good Friday. During the morning the people filed through the chapel 'Behind the Cross' (Egeria 37.13; in the Armenian Lectionary the atrium 'Before the Cross') to venerate the wood of the cross as well as several other relics. In the afternoon a three hours service was held in the atrium 'Before the Cross'. The service consisted of readings from the prophets, epistles, psalms, and all four passion narratives. Finally there was a service in the Anastasis to commemorate the burial of Jesus. Each of these three services was translated to the West and had a significant effect on Western liturgical practice.

---

[1] See Renoux, *Jer. Arm. 121*, p.269.
[2] See Gingras, *Egeria*, p.236.
[3] For the details of the service, see Baldovin, *Urban Character*, pp.61-62, 68-69, 94-96.
[4] See O. B. Hardison, *Christian Rite and Christian Drama in the Middle Ages*, (John Hopkins Univ. Press, Baltimore, 1965), pp.128-138.

3. The Great Vigil of Easter

The details of the development of the Paschal Vigil are far too complex to be done justice here.[1] Of course, as we have seen above, the solemn initiation of candidates took place during the vigil readings. As on Maundy Thursday a second celebration of the eucharist followed the one in the Martyrium, but in this instance at the Anastasis, perhaps as an expression of a desire to celebrate a particular mystery *in situ* with the eucharist.[2] The Old Testament vigil readings do call for some comment. Twelve readings were used as in the Epiphany vigil. Talley has suggested that they have not only typological but also eschatological overtones, in that the first three readings. Genesis 1, Genesis 22, and Exodus 12 refer to the Creation, the Sacrifice of Isaac, and the Passover, whereas the rest of the readings are eschatological. Thus the *cursus* of readings for the hagiopolite Paschal Vigil most probably reflects the 'Poem of the Four Nights,' in Targum Onkelos, in which the fourth night is that of final redemption.[3]

4. Easter Octave

The Easter octave is structured similarly to that of Epiphany. Once again the addition of the Martyrium of St. Stephen has caused the displacement of the Golgotha Martyrium, and the stations themselves reveal the reasoning behind the choice of lectionary readings. As with the Epiphany octave the gospels chosen for the week correspond to the theme of the celebration, in this case the resurrection narratives. The reading of Matthew 5.1-12 on Thursday, however, is a curious exception. Why would the beatitudes be read during the Easter octave? The answer of course can be found in the choice of stations. On Thursday of Easter week the station was the Eleona, atop the Mount of Olives. Clearly the church at Jerusalem related this mount to (at least the idea of) the mount where Jesus gave his famous sermon. Likewise the Letter of James (in addition to the Acts of the Apostles is read beginning on Wednesday. The Wednesday station is Sion, traditional seat of James, the first bishop of Jerusalem. Thus the hagiopolite church connected its celebration of the most solemn period of the year with readings from its own first leader. The choice of another odd reading, the Prologue of John's Gospel, on the Octave Sunday was probably not related so much to the station (the Martyrium) as to a desire to capture the whole sweep of salvation history at this solemn time.

5. The Fortieth Day After Easter

Egeria's description (42) of a special service on the Fortieth Day after Easter at Bethlehem has puzzled scholars.[4] Since she claims the celebration is appropriate

---

[1] For an extensive treatment, see Bertoniere, *Greek Easter Vigil,* esp. pp.7-105; also J. B. Thibaut, *L'ordre des offices de la semaine sainte à Jérusalem de IVme au Xme siècle,* (Paris, 1926), pp.114-127.

[2] See Bertoniere, *Greek Easter Vigil,* p.70.

[3] See Talley, *Origins,* pp.48-51.

[4] For the literature and further treatment, see Baldovin, *Uban Character,* pp.87-90.

to the time and place, it seems she must be referring to some reason for celebrating the Ascension at Bethlehem. It seems more likely that she has confused a date in the calendar (the slaughter of the Innocents, which falls in May in the Armenian Lectionary) with a date related to Easter.[1] Moreover, in the late fourth century the Ascension was commemorated on the afternoon of Pentecost Sunday at Jerusalem. It is not until the fifth century Armenian Lectionary that we find the tradition of the Ascension according to the Lucan chronology on the fortieth day after Easter. Again we must note that the fourth and fifth century liturgical calendar of Jerusalem was in a state of considerable flux.

6. Pentecost

Egeria notes (43.19) that Pentecost is a major feast of the hagiopolite liturgical year. The services which include a morning eucharist at the Martyrium, a second eucharist at Sion (site of the Holy Spirit's descent),an afternoon service at the Eleona (to commemorate the Ascension) and finally a procession after vespers to the major holy sites (Martyrium, Anastasis, Sion) in the city. Egeria claims that the day's liturgy ends only at midnight. The transfer of the Ascension to the fortieth day after Easter in the Armenian Lectionary results in a shift of focus for the Pentecost afternoon service at Eleona. Here it marks a solemn conclusion (with kneeling for the first time since Easter) to the season of rejoicing. Fasting, of course, resumes with this period to the Easter season.

7. Saints' Days

Except for the Feast of Encainia Egeria provides little information as to other feasts celebrated in the course of the hagiopolite year.[2] The Armenian Lectionary, on the other hand lays out some twenty-six special days.

In contrast with the list of saints in the Roman Philocalian Calendar (or the Chronograph of 354)[3], the Armenian Lectionary lays out a broad spectrum of types of saints and feasts. In the latter one finds: Hypapante (the Fortieth Day after Epiphany, mentioned above), Encainia (the Dedication of the Golgotha complex, 13 September with its octave), a feast of the miraculous apparition of the Cross (7 May), the Holy Innocents (9 or 18 May depending on the manuscript), a feast of the Virgin Mary (15 August), a feast of John the Baptist (29 August), a feast of the Ark of the Covenant (2 July), one confessor (Antony), two bishops (Cyril and John), two emperors (Constantine and Theodosius), seven Old Testament figures (Jeremiah, Zechariah, Elisha, the Maccabees, Isaiah, Jacob, and David), two feasts of martyrs (the Forty Martyrs of Sebaste and Stephen), and five commemorations of apostles (Thomas, Philip, Andrew, Peter and Paul, James and John).

---

[1] See the classic article by Georg Krestchmar, 'Himmelfahrt und Pfingsten', *Zeitschrift für Kirchengeschichte* 66 (1955), pp.209-253.

[2] She does, however, mention that there is no fasting on a Wednesday (and presumably a Friday) in Lent when that day coincides with a martyr's day (27:5); therefore she is familiar with saints' days.

[3] See H. Stern, *Le calendrier de 354*, (Paris, 1963).

Clearly by the early fifth century, at least at Jerusalem, there were a number of types of liturgical feasts. Each order (or *canon*) has a date, stational notice, and assigned readings. Presumably each included the celebration of the eucharist, which at Jerusalem, therefore, was celebrated on Sundays, Saturdays, Wednesdays and Fridays (except during Lent) and feast days. The number of feasts was vastly increased in the stage represented by the Georgian Lectionary, so that almost every day of the year had a commemoration of some sort.[1] It is possible that many of the Armenian Lectionary's feasts were not at all hagiopolite in origin but rather stemmed from even more primitive Palestinian tradition, as Kretschmar has argued.[2] Moreover, Kretschmar has revived the theory of H. Goussen that the Jerusalem church practiced *Gegendatierung*; i.e. 'paired-dating' by which certain feasts found their echo six months later.[3] For example, the counterpart of Stephen (27 Dec.) would be Zechariah (27 June); of Epiphany (6 Jan.) Isaiah (6 July); and of Hypapante (14 February) the Virgin Mary (15 Aug.). These pairs represent either extraordinary coincidence or a certain sense of balance in the mentality of the church that originated the feasts.

In conclusion we shall examine three hagiopolite feasts that influenced later Christianity. The exercise of such influence provides a fitting conclusion to our study as a whole. On August 15 the *canon* (order) of the Armenian Lectionary is entitled. 'Mary, Theotokos, at the Second Mile from Bethlehem.'[4] The date of the feast apparently derives from the dedication of a church in honour of Mary, constructed during the episcopate of Juvenal (422-458) at a spot recalling the 'resting' of Mary on her journey to Bethlehem in the *Protoevangelion of James*. The theme of the feast seems to have been the motherhood of Mary and not her dormition.[5] It was not long before the community made a mental leap from Mary's resting to her falling asleep (death). Thus sometime after the end of the fifth century the Georgian Lectionary witnesses to the same feast, but now celebrated at the site of Mary's tomb in Gethsemane.[6] Moreover the gospel reading was changed from the nativity of Jesus (Lk. 2.17) to the meeting of Mary and Elizabeth (Lk. 1.39-56). The title in the Georgian Lectionary remains that of a 'generic' feast of Mary, but now the station suggests a different theme, her dormition.

---

[1] See Tarchnisvili, *Grand Lectionnaire*, II:2.
[2] See Kretschmmar, 'Frühe Geschicte,' p.45, see also *idem.*, 'Festkalendar und Memorialstätten', pp.167-174.
[3] Kretschmar, 'Frühe Geschichte', pp.41ff. See Heinrich Goussen, *Uber georgische Drucke und Handschriften die Festirdung und den Heiligenkalender des altchristlichen Jerusalems betreffend*, (Munich, 1923).
[4] Renoux, *Cod. Jer. Arm. 121*, p.355.
[5] See J. Crehan, 'The Assumption and the Jerusalem Liturgy', in *Theolgical Studies* 30 (1969), pp.312-325.
[6] The Georgian Lectionary frequently abbreviates services or changes stations to sites nearer the city. For further comment, see Baldovin, *Urban Character*, pp.97-100.

A second feast of Mary that finds its origin in the Jerusalem church is that of the Presentation of the Virgin in the Temple (Nov. 21). This feast is not found in the Armenian but only in the Georgian Lectionary.[1] It commemorates the dedication of Justinian's New Church (*Nea*) of the Virgin Mary located near the old Temple Platform. Proximity to the Temple ruins probably inspired adopting the apocryphal legend of Mary's presentation as a child in the Temple (once again taken from the *Protoevangelion of James*). It makes little sense to translate feasts of dedication to other cities, but themes travel well and thus this feast became popular at first in the East and only later in the Middle Ages in the West.[2]

Encainia, the final feast on which we comment, brings us back full circle to our introduction. Egeria writes of this feast of the dedication of the Golgotha complex as one of the most important of the year, so important that it includes an octave. Perhaps the date was chosen because on it the true cross was discovered and it marked the dedication of Solomon's temple as she claims (48.12). It certainly coincided with the Roman dedication of the Temple of Jupiter Capitolinus. According to the Armenian Lectionary the true cross is shown to the people on the second day of the feast (14 September). Hence is derived the feast of the Triumph of the Cross, still celebrated today. That a feast so local in origin should profoundly influence the liturgical calendar and thus Christian spirituality should not surprise us. It merely confirms Jerusalem's tremendous symbolic and liturgical influence that we have seen throughout this study.

---

[1] Tarchnisvili, *Grand Lectionnaire II:2*, p.52.
[2] On how feasts which are originally local are eventually universalized by means of a calendar, see Jonathon Z. Smith, *To Take Place*, pp.96-117.

Alcuin/GROW Joint Liturgical Studies

All cost £2.75 in 1989

1987 TITLES

1. **(LS 49) Daily and Weekly Worship—from Jewish to Christian**
   by Roger Beckwith, Warden of Latimer House, Oxford
   Christianity arose in a Jewish context, and Christian worship bears marks of the fact. This becomes clearest when Jewish worship of the first century is investigated, so far as evidence allows, and is compared with primitive Christian worship. This Study concentrates on daily and weekly worship. It is now in a second edition.

2. **(LS 50) The Canons of Hippolytus**
   edited by Paul Bradshaw, Professor of Liturgics, University of Notre Dame
   These Canons, only available in manuscript in Arabic, reflect a Greek original which has been variously dated by scholars, but is here located in the early fourth century. This makes it the earliest source of Hippolytus himself.

3. **(LS 51) Modern Anglican Ordination Rites**
   edited by Colin Buchanan, Bishop of Aston
   The revisions of the last 15 years throughout the Anglican Communion are collected and presented by Colin Buchanan here done for ordination rites what he has done three times in the last decades for eucharistic rites.

4. **(LS 52) Models of Liturgical Theology**
   by James Empereur, of the Jesuit School of Theology, Berkeley
   Worship may be characterized differently, depending on the dominant model at work, such as liturgy as institution, as mystery, as sacrament, as proclamation, as process, as therapeutic, and as liberation. No one model exhausts the meaning of the liturgy; no one model can be omitted from an adequate theological understanding of the worship of the assembly.

1988 TITLES

5. **(LS 53) A Kingdom of Priests: Liturgical Formation of the Laity: The Brixen Essays**
   edited by Thomas Talley, Professor of Liturgics, General Theological Seminary, New York.
   This volume is a thoroughly edited collection of the salient papers read at the second international Anglican Liturgical Consultation held at Brixen in Northern Italy in August 1987—and, from America, Britain, and Africa alike, they combine planning aspects of the liturgy to-day in Anglicanism with the 'results' in terms of the building up of the laity.

6. **(LS 54) The Bishop in Liturgy: an Anglican Study**
   edited by Colin Buchanan, Bishop of Aston
   This symposium begins from a paper of Colin Buchanan, delivered at the Brixen Consultation but deliberately excluded from Study no. 5 summarized above. Some treatment of history, of pastoral considerations, and of expectations varying from diocese to diocese and continent to continent, leads on into practical help for bishops and for all those who welcome bishops to minister in their parishes or larger contexts.

7. **(LS 55) Inculturation: the Eucharist in Africa**
   by Phillip Tovey, research student, previously tutor in liturgy in Uganda
   The author draws upon broad study and also his own experience in Africa to illustrate the principle of inculturation concerning the relating of liturgy to local culture in Africa.

8. **(LS 56) Essays in Early Eastern Initiation**
   edited by Paul Bradshaw, Professor of Liturgics, University of Notre Dame
   A well-known editor from the Church of England, a professor at Notre Dame University, presents three authors who open up new issues and provide new theories in relation to the early Eastern baptismal rites.

1989 TITLES

9. **(LS 57) The Liturgy of the Church in Jerusalem**
   by John Baldovin (March 1989)

10. **(LS 58) Adult Initiation**
    edited by Donald Withey (June 1989)
    This is a collection of the papers read at the Society for Liturgical Study in Summer 1988.

11. **(LS 59) The Contents of the Early Antiochene Anaphora**
    by John Fenwick (September 1989)

12. **(LS 60) Calvin and Bullinger on the Lord's Supper**
    by Paul Rorem (December 1989)